PRAISING THE GIFTS OF GOD

Other Citadel Books by Allan A. Swenson

Plants of the Bible and How to Grow Them

Flowers of the Bible and How to Grow Them

Herbs of the Bible and How to Grow Them

PRAISING THE GIFTS OF GOD

Allan A. Swenson

CITADEL PRESS
Kensington Publishing Corp.
www.kensingtonbooks.com

CITADEL PRESS BOOKS are published by

Kensington Publishing Corp.
850 Third Avenue
New York, NY 10022

All Kensington titles, imprints, and distributed lines are available at special quantity discounts for bulk purchases for sales promotions, premiums, fund-raising, educational, or institutional use. Special book excerpts or customized printings can also be created to fit specific needs. For details, write or phone the office of the Kensington special sales manager: Kensington Publishing Corp., 850 Third Avenue, New York, NY 10022, attn: Special Sales Department; phone: 1-800-221-2647.

CITADEL PRESS and the Citadel logo are Reg. U.S. Pat. & TM Off.

First Printing: September 2005
First paperback printing: September 2006

10 9 8 7 6 5 4 3 2 1

Printed in the United States of America

Library of Congress Control Number: 2005922711

ISBN 0-8065-2763-3

To All Christians everywhere.
May the light of Jesus shine ever brightly
in your hearts and his teaching be
an ongoing guide for your lives.

Contents

Acknowledgments

This book has been one of the most challenging I've ever written. It required long hours, weeks, and months of thought after visiting in person and via the wonders of telephone and e-mail with more people than can be listed here. This book began decades ago while learning lessons in Sunday School in the Garden State of New Jersey, so my heartfelt thanks to those dedicated teachers who implanted vital Christian concepts and knowledge in my mind so many years ago. And also to others who have provided inspiration with their worthwhile ideas, advice, sermons, and counsel through the years, as well as by their personal examples of Christian faith and living.

Thanks also must go to the builders of churches, the artists who adorned them and even the faithful workers who clean and tend houses of worship. All are part of our shared heritage. Salutes also are deserved by the legions of greeters, ushers, and young acolytes who serve their parishes and congregations. I gladly offer thanks to those who cook church suppers, teach youngsters, practice what they preach, and guide our footsteps along the pathway of Christianity. Praises are deserved by organists and choirs, musicians and musical directors who glorify God with sacred music of yesterday and today. In truth, all Christians rightfully should be acknowledged. Each in his or her own way carries forward the faith for the world to see.

Special personal thanks to the inspiration in my life, my beloved wife, Sheila, and to Rev. Lamar Robinson, his daughter, the late Amy Robinson, and my devout cousin, Amy Tudor Dugdale Luciano, for their insights and examples of faith over the years. And to other special people like Gordon Miller, John Durgin, Brother Edmund, and Brother Marcel, my thanks for forthright answers to questions and for your friendship.

I could not have written this book without the quality of the contribution I got from Nancy Gratton, who stepped in as a master collaborator, researcher, and editor. As always, many thanks to my agent, Jake Elwell, and to the Citadel editors Bob Shuman, Amanda Rouse, and Steven M. Long. Thanks also to Bruce Bender and Mary Russell.

Writing my *Plants of the Bible* book and doing Holy Land slide shows also allowed me to meet many dedicated Christian gardeners who faithfully grow glorious Biblical gardens at their homes and churches, and in their communities. Many thanks for their efforts and the joys those give to others. And to all those who beautify local churches for Sunday services and special events.

While giving talks about my Biblical plant books in a number of places, from small rural churches to the Cathedral Church of St. John the Divine, I have learned many lessons in life that I trust have found their way into this book too. To each and everyone who has given of him- or herself to further our Christian faith, profuse thanks and best wishes, as we all do our part in following and spreading the gospel of Jesus Christ.

Introduction: Praising the Gifts of God

The history and heritage of Christianity is ancient, yet it is as vital and vibrant today as it was when the first followers of Christ set forth to build His church. For more than two millenia, followers of Jesus Christ have spread the Gospel of His coming and His teachings and today number more than 2 billion worldwide. Christian worship can take many different forms, and individuals who profess Christianity may belong to a wide variety of denominations. But all share one fundamental item of faith: that Jesus Christ came to us to cleanse us of our sins and that only through faith in Him can we find our way to salvation.

Christianity is, first and foremost, a matter of religious faith. But the history of the Christian movement has given the world so much more. The influence of Christianity can be seen in the founding documents of the American nation. It has molded and shaped our artistic aesthetic. It inspires our civil life and even the meanings we attach to home and family. It is a fundamental part of how we look at the world, providing us with our most profoundly held values. It provides us with the spiritual framework according to which we make sense of our lives.

Because Christianity is such an essential part of our culture, we sometimes take for granted its many manifestations, large and small, in our daily lives. Still, whether we realize it or not, we celebrate our Christian heritage every day. From the currency we carry in our pockets to the best of the music that sustains us, we pass the message of Christ's salvation throughout our lives.

How much better it would be if we fully recognized the breadth and depth of this heritage! That is the goal of this book: to share the history and meaning of the Christian heritage in all aspects of our lives. We will explore the ways in which Christianity has influenced our art, music, and literature. We will learn about the great men and women who helped spread the Word and established our churches. We will revisit the sites where Christianity first flowered, and we will explore the fundamental contribution of Christianity to the formation of our own nation.

Christianity, in all its denominational diversity, grants its believers a path to salvation, and along the way it offers innumerable joys, born of a life lived in emulation of the Lord. Every day, we are granted the opportunity for small, private celebrations of faith, in a world filled with reminders of Christ's love. When we contemplate our nation's heritage, when we see our faith and values represented in the masterpieces of Christian-inspired art and music, when we give of ourselves in charitable works—in all these ways, we grow in faith.

The more we know about our own Christian heritage, the better we will be able to appreciate its gifts. As we go about our daily lives, we will be better able to appreciate—and yes, celebrate—the great gift of faith that was born more than 2,000 years ago in the dusty little town of Bethlehem. In the pages to follow, I offer you a small sampling of the myriad ways that our Christian heritage has enriched all our lives.

I

ART AND ARCHITECTURE

The influence of Christianity in the arts has been profound. Beginning with the verbal arts, as found in the lyrical passages of scripture handed down to us from the early disciples, it has emerged in every form of creative expression devised by humankind and informed by the faithful spirit. Today, Christianity finds expression not only in the written word and the performing and visual arts but also in the modern industries that support these endeavors. In all these venues, the message of Christianity, its values and its traditions, have been celebrated throughout the high and popular cultures of every era.

The inspiration of Christ's life can be found depicted in works of great art, from Michelangelo's haunting sculpture, the Pièta *(1498–1499), to the devotionally inspired architecture of churches.*

It is equally found in the rousing strains of gospel music and in the powerful cinematic images of Mel Gibson's The Passion of the Christ *(2004). Throughout our culture and history, creativity and the human spirit have forged together to produce vibrant, living testimony to the promise of faith and hope embodied in Christ's example and the religious faith that bears His name.*

Visual Arts

From the earliest times, Christian artists turned to their faith for inspiration. In fact, during the first centuries of Christianity, when the profession of Christian faith was tantamount to treason against Rome, symbolic art was one of the few means by which Christians could give public testimony to their beliefs. Not all early Christians approved of visual representation of religious themes, however, because there was a tradition, inherited from the laws of Moses, that spoke against the creation of graven images.

Nonetheless, symbolic images appeared in the first three centuries of Christianity—images that did not rely on what could be considered idolatrous commemoration of individuals, but that held profound religious meaning to adherents of the Christian faith. Among the more ubiquitous of these early images is the simple line drawing of the fish. This became something of an emblem and secret sign of Christianity, because the Greek word for *fish* (*ichthus*) served as an acronym for Christ Himself: *Iesus, CHristos, THeus* (of God), *Uiou* (the Son), and

Soter (Savior). This acronym, like a secret password, had further implications for devout Christians because of its scriptural relevance, for in Mark 1:17 Jesus tells His disciples, "Follow me, and I will make you fishers of men." More open representations of Christ and His mission could only be found in hidden spaces, such as the catacombs of Rome, where frescoes depicting scenes from the life of Christ could be painted in secret.

With the conversion of the Roman emperor Constantine to Christianity, the representation of Christian themes in sculpture and painting no longer needed to be kept hidden. When Christianity became the state religion of Rome in A.D. 313, an efflorescence of religiously themed art occurred. The art of this period, which spans from 313 through the middle of the 1400s, is called Byzantine, because it was influenced by the styles current in the eastern part of the empire, which was centered in Byzantium. Nonetheless, the forms and styles of artistic expression underwent great changes over the course of the Byzantine era.

Great Christian mosaic art began in the fourth century and was largely restricted to church settings. This was a time of great church building, and in the churches of the time (called *basilicas*) sequences of mosaic panels ran the length of the nave (where the congregants stood) and decorated the area above the columns that supported the church ceiling. These mosaics commonly depicted scenes from the Old Testament, such as the delivery of the Ten Commandments by Moses, or they drew on the life of Christ and His apostles. During this period, direct depictions of Christ in His ministry, and of Mary, His mother, were another increasingly common theme.

It can be said that, until the 1400s, nearly all Western visual art was Christian art, because the most powerful patrons of the art were either the Church of Rome, or the European ruling houses, which were themselves allied with Rome. And perhaps the greatest of all the artists subsidized by the church was Michelangelo. His artistic legacy to us, from the tragic yet ultimately hopeful image of Mary cradling the body of her crucified son (*Pieta*, 1498–1499) to the majestic frescoes of the Sistine Chapel (*The Creation and the Fall*, on the ceiling, was painted from 1508 to 1512; *The Last Judgement*, behind the altar, was painted from 1535 to 1541).

At the end of the 1400s, a movement arose in Europe to break the Roman monopoly over the profession of Christianity. This was the Reformation (1450–1550), during which new voices rose up against the established church, led by such figures as Martin Luther and John Calvin. Calvin, in particular, is associated with the rejection of Roman-influenced religious art, which he denounced as idolatrous iconography. But the movements did not condemn all art. Rather, this period saw the introduction of new, less exalted and more mundane themes. Jesus and His disciples were still depicted, but no longer as elite lords. Rather, they were incorporated into scenes that resonated with the lives of ordinary people.

The artists of this time rejected what they called the artificial segregation of the sacred and the secular, recalling that Jesus came to save the common folk—the poor and the powerless—and that He served as a living reminder that the ordinary life was as legitimate a glorification of

God as the life of any powerful ruler. Artists such as Hieronymus Bosch (1450–1516) depicted humanity's vulnerability to temptation. Albrecht Durer (1471–1528) worked in the Renaissance style, and his greatest works were drawn from the Bible. Chief among his legacy to us are the woodcuts known as the "Apocalypse Series," which illustrate the Revelations of Saint John.

The distinction between Protestant Christian art and the art patronized by the Roman church that arose in the Reformation era reflected a fundamental difference in philosophy. For both sides of the debate, however, the celebration of faith in everyday life has become an important theme—perhaps the most important theme—in Christian art today.

Church Architecture

Early Christians worshipped in secret. As a persecuted sect within the Roman Empire, they faced imprisonment for treason if they were found practicing their faith. For three centuries, there were no formal houses of Christian worship. Instead, Christians gathered in small groups of close friends and family members to conduct their religious ceremonies. It was not until A.D. 313, when the Roman emperor Constantine converted, that the profession of Christian faith was made lawful and Christians were allowed to profess their faith publicly.

The earliest churches were simple, rectangular buildings that housed an altar at one end, behind which was built a rounded alcove called an *apse*. With Constantine's conversion to the faith, pagan temples began to be converted for use as houses of Christian worship, and the first elaboration of Christian architecture was begun. As the church gained in converts and thus in influence, church architectural style became more elaborate, and certain structures within the churches became standard.

The basic internal structure of a church consists of two parts. First is the *chancel*, which holds the altar and apse, and from which the services are conducted. Second, but equally important, is the *nave*, where the congregation is seated. The chancel is generally elevated by at least a step or two from the nave. Together, these two elements are often called the *sanctuary*. Within the chancel, and to the right side, is the pulpit. This may be a simple reader's stand or it may be a more ornate, impressively elevated affair. This is where the Gospel is read, and thus this side of the church is frequently known as "the Gospel side." Opposite the pulpit but still within the chancel is another reading stand, called the *lectern*, on which a Bible traditionally rests open. This is for the use of a lay person from the congregation, who reads from the Old Testament or, often, from the Epistles of the New Testament. This is called the "Epistle side."

The nave, where the congregation sits, was once a simple open space, and worshippers stood to pray. During the medieval period, however, this area was fitted with plain or high-backed benches, called *pews*, before each of which were placed padded *kneelers*. In many churches, the pews all face forward, toward the altar, but in some the pews are set along the walls, at right angles to the altar, so that half of the congregation faces the other half.

Two other elements were added during the medieval period and remain in use today. The first is the *sacristy*, in which communion equipment and vestments for the priest or minister are kept. The second is the *narthex*, which is a separate foyer. The narthex was traditionally a low, narrow entryway, symbolizing the solitary passage of the individual soul into the state of grace.

Over the course of the centuries, these essential elements of the Christian house of worship underwent elaboration. Saint Peter's Basilica in Rome was built by Giacomo della Porta over a twenty-year period, from 1546 to 1564, and is a glorious example of the Italian Renaissance style of architecture. Westminster Abbey, built in the thirteenth century by England's King Henry III on the site of an older, Norman church, reflects the then novel style of architecture known as Gothic. Its limestone and marble has been host to the coronation of every British monarch since it was first constructed in the early 1200s.

The elaborate church styles favored by the medieval church and retained in many later Catholic houses of worship incorporated a variety of other forms of art, from statues of saints to stained-glass depictions of the Stations of the Cross. Some include additional elements, such as "ladies' chapels" or shrines dedicated to specific devotions. Cathedrals, which are presided over by bishops (as in the Catholic and Episcopalian denominations), are frequently very elaborate and incorporate within the chancel a special chair, called the *cathedra*, on which the bishop sits.

In America, the early Protestant churches adopted a simpler, meeting-hall style. Steeples were a common feature, often housing a bell or bells with which the congregation was called to prayer. By the 1600s, some denominations had swung toward opulence once again, and the frame and clapboard structures of the more austere Puritan sects were replaced in some areas by more impressive edifices of dressed stone. In the early twentieth century, the trend in Protestant church architecture was again toward simpler lines, and some denominations adopted the style employed by architect Frank Lloyd Wright in his Unity Temple (1904).

Christian Films

Although the advent of filmmaking dates to the 1890s, it would be half a century before a specifically Christian filmmaking movement could get its start. For one thing, it took until the 1930s for filmmaking to move from the status of curiosity to cultural phenomenon. For another, the early film studios controlled both production and distribution and saw no profit in marketing many specifically Christian-themed films. In addition, many churches viewed films solely in terms of what they saw emanating from the major film companies of the era and wanted nothing to do with the product.

In the 1940s, however, all this changed. One of the earliest pioneers in the Christian film movement was Maxwell A. Kerr. Drawn to filmmaking from early childhood, Kerr took a part-time job during his high school years as a projectionist to learn the process from the ground up. He received the call to Christ in 1937, and it was only natural for him to turn to his first vocational love, film, as a way to spread his newfound faith. He felt certain that film was a powerful medium to spread the

Word of the Gospel and searched until he discovered the Baptista Film Ministry, a small production company that was founded by Charles Octavia Baptista, a Latin American immigrant and Christian convert.

Through the Baptista Film Ministry, some of the earliest gospel-themed movies (mostly animated) were made. The company marketed directly to churches, guaranteeing the content of its films and offering discount packages that included both the projector equipment and a selection of film titles. One of its very first products was an allegorical animated short, *The Story of a Fountain Pen* (1940). Kerr worked as a technological consultant and didn't join the company until six years later, when Baptista Film Ministry hired him on full time to develop a sound-and-image projection system. The company soon moved from moving pictures to the production of educational filmstrips, however.

Another pioneer was Ken Anderson, who began in Christian publishing but, in 1949, decided to explore the possibilities of filmmaking. He created a film studio, Gospel Films, and developed his own distribution division. He was joined in the early 1950s by Dick Ross, who created a documentary film on Billy Graham's evangelical ministry. Graham quickly recognized the potential of film as an evangelical adjunct and created World Wide Pictures with the express aim of producing and distributing Christian-themed films. The new company employed both Anderson and Ross in creative positions.

In 1960, Anderson left World Wide Pictures to create his own production company, Ken Anderson Films. His first film remains his most celebrated—a film version of John Bunyan's *Pilgrim's Progress* (1979), in the making of which he drew on the talents of Kerr, among others, and in which Liam Neeson had his first film role.

Throughout the 1940s, 1950s, and 1960s, Christian films suffered from the reluctance of mainstream movie theaters to accept specifically gospel-oriented films. While the occasional Hollywood blockbuster would receive wide general screenings, most Christian films were limited to distribution among church groups, which would rent the films for limited audiences. It wasn't until the 1970s that Christian filmmakers broke through the invisible barrier that kept them from a broader viewership. It was Graham's World Wide Pictures that led the way. In partnership with major churches across America, they formed Gateway Films, which produced the classic movie *The Cross and the Switchblade* (1970), starring Pat Boone.

The succsss of Gateway Films inspired others to establish specifically Christian film production companies over the next two decades. The Kuntz Brothers (*Dakota*, 1988), Trinity Broadcasting (*China Cry*, 1990), and Canadian-based Cloud Ten Pictures (*Left Behind*, 2001) all achieved general theatrical release and found wide audience acceptance.

By the 1990s, however, these advances were offset by the loss of the traditional venue for Christian films. Churches no longer seemed interested in serving as film outlets, and rentals for church showings dropped off precipitously. This led to the closing of a number of Christian film libraries, which depended on their church clientele for revenues. Christian filmmaking was poised to go mainstream and was new-technology (especially DVD) friendly, so the demand for older films, particularly those made with older 16 mm technologies, declined dramatically.

In 1992, the first explicitly Christian film festival was founded by Tom Saab in Salem, New Hampshire. His Merrimack Valley Christian Film Festival, hosted during Easter Week, offered wide public viewings of Christian-themed films, followed by a gospel presentation and a call to the altar. His success encouraged the establishment of the WYSIWYG (What You See Is What You Get) Film Festival in San Francisco in 1999 and the Dama Film Festival in Seattle, Washington.

Good News from Hollywood

Although explicitly Christian cinema did not "get off the ground" until the 1940s, and the widespread theatrical distribution of Christian films had to wait until the 1990s, this did not mean that Hollywood entirely failed to produce Christian-themed films, even during its earliest years. From the era of silent films, when King Vidor and Cecil B. DeMille began the genre of the Bible epic, to director Mel Gibson's *The Passion of the Christ* (2004), filmmakers have been drawn to both the Old and New Testaments for inspiration.

Hollywood has traditionally produced three types of biblically inspired films: Old Testament stories, the life and times of Jesus Christ, and the sometimes disparagingly called "sword and sandal" epics, which deal with the early Christian converts during the era of Roman prosecution. The first type was also the first to be represented in film by director D. W. Griffith in 1914. His film, the Old Testament epic *Judith of Bethulia*, was not, strictly speaking, an Old Testament film. Rather, it was based on one of the books of Apocrypha. It featured the silent stars

Lillian Gish and Lionel Barrymore and cost an extraordinary (for the time) $35,000 to make.

DeMille, another prominent director of the silent era, found the Bible a perfect source of inspiration for the kind of stories he most loved to tell: epic in scope, with a strong moral core. His early efforts focused on the Old Testament, which has proven to be a fertile source of inspiration for filmmakers from the silent era to the present. One of the earliest ever made was the 1923 silent-film classic *The Ten Commandments*. DeMille attempted to make the biblical lesson relevant to contemporary life by intertwining the story of Moses with the tale of a 1920s widow who uses Bible readings to instill in her sons the values of the Ten Commandments.

DeMille turned again to the Old Testament for inspiration in 1949, when he directed *Samson and Delilah* (starring Hedy Lamarr and Victor Mature). Other important films of the genre are *David and Bathsheba* (1951), directed by Henry King and starring Gregory Peck and Susan Hayward; King Vidor's *Soloman and Sheba* (1959), starring Yul Brynner and Gina Lollobrigida; DeMille's 1956 remake of *The Ten Commandments*, with a huge cast that included Charlton Heston as Moses and many of the other major stars of the day, from Brynner and Edward G. Robinson to Yvonne De Carlo and Anne Baxter. In 1962, director Robert Aldrich put together an international cast led by the American actor Stewart Granger (who played Lot) for his film *Sodom and Gomorrah*.

More ambitious was the simply titled John Huston film *The Bible*, which was released in 1966 and attempted to relate the book of Genesis from Creation to the Flood. His film, like DeMille's *Ten Commandments*, called on the talents of many of the top stars of the 1960s, including George C. Scott, Ava Gardner, Stephen Boyd, and Peter O'Toole. The story of Moses was taken up again in 1975, when director Gianfranco De Bosio released *Moses the Lawgiver*, starring Burt Lancaster. In a class of its own is a musical treatment of an Old Testament story that found popular acceptance on the stage during the 1980s and the big screen in the late 1990s. This was *Joseph and the Amazing Technicolor Dreamcoat*, starring Donny Osmond, and marked the first collaboration of Andrew Lloyd Webber and Tim Rice. Nearly unique among Bible films, it was a full-scale musical and spawned a very popular soundtrack album of contemporary pop tunes.

With one exception, Hollywood postponed the production of movies that drew on the life and times of Jesus in the 1950s, in part because studios were nervous about how best to handle the depiction of Jesus without offending religious sensibilities. The exception was the 1927 silent classic *King of Kings*, another DeMille film. After nearly eighty years, the film still has a strong following and is frequently shown by missionaries in the field even today. In 1961, Nicholas Ray directed a remake of this powerful story, casting Jeffrey Hunter in the lead role. In 1965, director George Stevens took up the challenge, casting Max von Sydow as Jesus in *The Greatest Story Ever Told*. A decade later, in 1977, Franco Zeffirelli directed the sensitive, if somewhat controversial *Jesus of Nazareth*, starring Robert Powell and Anne Bancroft. Perhaps the most unusual approach taken in the telling of the story of Jesus can be found in David Greene's *Godspell* (1973), which transposed the Gospel of Mark to the streets of Manhattan and told the story in song. That same year saw the release of Norman Jewison's *Jesus Christ Superstar*, another musical but one that retained the historical setting and personages familiar from the Bible. Mel Gibson's 2004 release, *The Passion of the Christ*, is thus the inheritor of a long Hollywood tradition.

The final category of Hollywood films with biblical themes contains movies that attempt to portray the early church during Roman persecution, from the viewpoint of Christian converts. Perhaps the best known of these films is William Wyler's *Ben-Hur* (1959), starring Charlton Heston. While it is set during Jesus's lifetime, its focus is on the dawn of faith in the hearts of those who heard His teachings. Wyler based his epic on a much earlier, silent film of the same name, directed by Fred Niblo and released in 1925. Other films of this type include *The Sign of the Cross* (1932), another DeMille film, starring Fredric March and Claudette Colbert; *Quo Vadis?* (1951), starring Robert Taylor, Deborah Kerr, and Peter Ustinov and directed by Mervyn LeRoy; *The Robe* (1953), starring Richard Burton and directed by Henry Koster; and *Barabbas* (1962), starring Anthony Quinn and directed by Richard Fleischer.

Today, the production of religiously themed films for broad theatrical release no longer depends on Hollywood. Independent film production companies with the explicit mission of producing Christian films came into their own in the 1990s. Intent on making films that could speak to the wider public and so spread the Gospel message, Mark IV Pictures began making a name for itself by producing Hollywood-quality films with a distinctly Christian emphasis. Best known for its series of end-time films, based on Revelations, it has achieved a level of success that rivals any of the secular independent film companies.

Gospel Music

Gospel music emerged from the slave quarters of the American South, where African musical traditions merged with the hymnal traditions of American Protestantism. Inspired by the messages brought to them by itinerant preachers and the "praise houses" of the plantation, slaves expressed their spiritual longings in music, as they had been accustomed to do in their homelands.

Fearing the prospect of rebellion, slaveowners generally prohibited drumming and dancing in the slave quarters. Thus, slaves had to keep this form of religious expression secret. The spirituals they created during these early years were sung outside of the mainstream churches. They were sung a capella or to a rudimentary beat provided by clapping hands.

By the mid-1800s, this music had grown to include a sizeable body of songs. They had passed into tradition, handed down from generation to generation, but never written down. With the abolition of slavery, these spiritual songs emerged from secrecy and began to be sung in churches and at the Christian revival meetings that sprang up throughout the South.

The spirituals of the plantations underwent a further development in the early decades of the twentieth century, when African American musicians began to receive recognition for the new musical forms they were creating—music that came to be known as blues and jazz. This new music drew the attention of Thomas Andrew Dorsey, the son of a revivalist preacher who embarked on a career in music under the stage name of "Georgia Tom." In 1910, he quickly made a name for himself in Atlanta, where he played piano at local honky-tonks. Soon, however, he branched out into composing and arranging, and when he moved to Chicago in the 1920s he honed his craft by attending the College of Composition and Arranging there.

After achieving success in blues and jazz, Dorsey felt the call to combine his blues-based musical sensibility with more spiritual themes. In 1932, following a profound personal loss, he was inspired to write his most famous song, "Precious Lord, Take My Hand." A few short years later, in 1937, he composed the almost equally famous "Peace in the Valley."

Dorsey's music was rejected by the mainstream Chicago churches at first, but he did not let this deter him. He eventually wrote more than 800 songs, and they were performed by such Gospel luminaries as Mahalia Jackson, James Cleveland, and Clara Ward and the Ward Singers.

Gospel music is a hybrid, combining the raw enthusiasm of early spirituals with the sophisticated rhythms of blues and jazz. The new music added an emotional dimension that was hitherto lacking in the then more conventional church music that was born of European traditions. Its performers soon brought the music beyond the doors of the church, introducing the broader popular culture to its prayerful energy. Through the work of quartets such as the Caravans, the Dixie Hummingbirds, the Fairfield Four, the Harmonettes, and the Swan Silvertones, and the solo artistry of Mahalia and Aretha Franklin, gospel singers gained international respect, and gospel music is now firmly established in American music.

Hymns and Carols

The tradition of hymns and praise songs dates back to the second century, when members of an early Christian sect known as the Gnostics accompanied the words of certain psalms with musical instrumentation. For the next several hundred years, this tradition of combining scripturally derived or inspired poetry with music continued in a variety of forms among the various competing sects throughout Christian Europe before the fall of the Roman Empire.

During the Middle Ages, the accumulated body of music, especially plainsong chants, were collected and codified. For several centuries, this repertory was added to and embellished with new compositions and musical techniques, but they shared the common trait of being composed in Latin, making them accessible to the religious of all nationalities. Intended as they were for performance during the celebration of Mass, these compositions were serious and deeply spiritual in theme and style. Among the hymn composers of this period were Ambrose of Milan (d. 397) and Hrabanus Maurus (d. 1400).

For most of this period, church music was largely inaccessible to the broader population. Meant to be sung as part of the church service and written in Latin, its very formality kept it a world apart from the common churchgoer. It didn't help much that the church was distinctly disapproving of the secular music of the time, so much so that at many times and in many places it actively attempted to suppress the performance of the music of the common people.

Meanwhile, a secular musical tradition was developing throughout feudal Europe of the eleventh and twelve centuries, exemplified by the troubadours and minstrels patronized by the lordly manors. These performers eventually left their exclusively courtly venues and began performing for the wider public, and by the fourteenth century they were familiar sights in taverns and town squares, and their songs touched on popular themes, from the seasonal demands of the harvest to tales of lost or unrequited love.

In the fourteenth century, the earliest popular hymns, Christmas carols, began to be performed. Although concerned with Christian themes, particularly the nativity of Jesus, they were meant to be sung outside the context of the church. From these early, seasonally specific works, it was only a short step to the congregational music that arose during the Renaissance era and drew on secular song styles popular in France, Italy, Germany, and Spain. The spread and popularity of this new music was greatly facilitated by the development of the printing press in the middle of the fifteenth century. With this new machine, the lyrics and music could be produced in mass quantities and everyone could learn to sing along.

In the early 1500s, Germany's Martin Luther called for reform of the church. His populist message earned him the enmity of the traditional church, but it led him to explore new ways of spreading the message of redemption and salvation. He composed some of the earliest hymns, including "From Heaven above to Earth I Come." He also collected traditional spiritual chorales and composed more on his own, publishing them for distribution to Lutheran churches as early as 1524.

In England during this same period, the well-known Christmas carols "Angels We Have Heard on High" and "Oh, Come, All Ye Faithful" were also written and enjoyed great popular acceptance. By the end of the 1500s, printed collections of hymns and carols were widely available throughout England and the European continent. At the same time, England's growing Calvinist movement began publishing collections of Psalms, called *psalters*, that were meant to be sung or chanted by the congregation. These provided the model for the first hymnals used in the Puritan colonies of North America.

Popular Music

The Christian influence has found its way even into the realm of contemporary popular music. The movement, dubbed "contemporary Christian music" (CCM) by music critic Ron Moore in 1976, actually got its start a few years previously. The music employs a wide range of contemporary styles, including pop, rock, rap, alternative, and even goth/punk, but the lyrics explicitly reference the teachings of Jesus and are intended as one more way to spread the word of the Gospels.

At the heart of the movement are two passages from Scripture. Ephesians 5:18–19 enjoins Christians to "be not drunk with wine, wherein is excess; but be filled with the Spirit; speaking to yourselves in psalms and hymns and spiritual songs, singing and making melody in your heart to the Lord." Colossians 3:16 tells us, "Let the word of Christ dwell in you richly . . . teaching and admonishing one another in psalms and hymns and spiritual songs, singing with grace in your hearts to the Lord." Exponents of CCM point to these verses as scriptural legitimation of their work.

Before the 1970s, there were a few popular music performers who recorded songs that were, in their view, compatible with their Christianity and expressive of their faith. Among the best known of these artists was Pat Boone, who bluntly declared his commitment to the faith and used his celebrity to witness for Christ. But mainstream music labels were interested in catching the popular fads of the day and made little effort to cultivate this musical genre. It wasn't until the 1970s, when several broadcasters rebelled against the increasingly profane secular music of the day, that new, specifically Christian radio stations began to appear. This, in turn, provided the incentive for new record labels to form—labels that devoted themselves specifically to the production and distribution of Christian music in all the popular styles of the day.

One of the pioneers of this form of music is Larry Norman, who made his solo album debut in 1969 with a collection of what he called "Jesus music." One of his early hits was "Upon This Rock." Frequently referred to as the "father of Christian music," he quickly developed a large and loyal fan base. Meanwhile, Randy Stonehill, a contemporary of Norman's, became a protégé of Boone, who helped him make his own debut album in 1971.

Just like their secular counterparts on the popular music scene, Christian artists needed the support of record labels and access to the airwaves. Among the very first specifically Christian record companies was Myrrh Records, founded in the early 1970s. In the 1980s and 1990s, the number of Christian record labels grew, adding Frontline Records, Exit Records, and Refuge Records to the roster, among many others.

Meanwhile, new radio stations featuring Christian music were adding to the ranks of preexisting broadcasters, which were traditionally gospel oriented but were now expanding to offer music from the broad popular spectrum.

The 1980s were a time of great crossover success by Christian artists. Performers like Amy Grant, Steven Curtis Chapman, and dc Talk were getting serious airplay, and Grant's music, in particular, found success even on the playlists of the secular broadcast stations. Today, Christian broadcasters number in the thousands across the country and have formed a professional organization, National Religious Broadcasters, to establish and maintain standards for Christian music of all kinds. At least one college (Central Christian College) even offers a two-year degree in CCM, with courses in everything from performance to music theory. In 1993, the CCM movement broke down a further barrier with the creation of a cable music station, Z-Music, that offered an MTV-like showcase for the music and videos of Christian popular artists.

The growth of CCM was not without controversy. Some church leaders, particularly among the more conservative, fundamentalist denominations, rejected the use of secular styles. Many artists were accused of trivializing Christ's message through weak or ambiguous lyrics. Other critics found contemporary musical styles inconsistent with spirituality. The heavy beat of rock, for instance, was condemned as being more appropriate to the excitement of the flesh than the edification of the spirit, however lofty the lyrics might be. One of the most vocal opponents to CCM is the Reverend Jimmy Swaggart, who has devoted several books to the subject.

As crossover onto mainstream radio playlists has become more and more common, some of the younger CCM artists have moved away from recording with the established Christian record labels. Citing frustration with the restrictions placed on them, performers like Leslie Phillips, who rose to prominence in the 1980s, formed their own independent labels to gain greater creative freedom.

Christian Publishing Today

Christianity has enjoyed a long, vibrant literary tradition, but it was only with the invention of the printing press that a true publishing industry could arise and flourish. Still, with rare exceptions, the tradition of Christian publishing has been one concerned with the production of Bibles, Bible study guides, missionary tracts, and other Bible-related items. In the major bookstores, religious-themed literature was usually granted limited shelf space, and to find Christian literature in any quantity and variety, a reader generally had to find a specialty store.

Beginning in the 1990s, however, a new trend began to gain momentum. The traditional publishers, such as Fortress Press and Randall House, continued in their tradition of producing quality Bibles and study guides, but others, like Bethany House, Multnomah Press, and Zandorvan began to explore the feasibility of expanding their scope to include fiction. A key figure in inspiring this new direction in publishing is Gilbert Morris, often credited with being the "father of Christian fiction."

Morris, a pastor and educator, began writing fiction with Christian themes in the 1990s through Bethany House. His works span several genres, from historical sagas to science fiction, but they are all fundamentally informed by a Christian ethic and celebrate Christian values. He set the standard for all Christian fiction to follow. Bethany House saw in his books the potential for expanding its market beyond the traditional Christian distribution chain and succeeded in getting his books carried by the major secular chains such as B. Dalton and Barnes and Noble. Morris's success led the industry as a whole to rethink its focus. Soon, several other houses began to look for quality fiction with Christian themes. Multnomah followed up with related titles.

Another traditional Christian publisher, Tyndale Press, found its own recipe for success when it contracted to publish a manuscript by an accidental pair of collaborators in 1995. Tim LeHaye was a sixty-something veteran of the Christian political movement known as the Moral Majority with little fiction writing experience. Jerry B. Jenkins was a much younger man who had been earning his living ghostwriting autobiographies of major sports celebrities. They were paired up when LaHaye found himself unable to bring to life a story idea that struck him while aboard an airplane. LaHaye's agent, who also handled Jenkins's books, suggested a collaboration, then sold the results of their joint labors to Tyndale. With this, the novel *Left Behind* was born, launching the wildly successful series about the end-time. Sixty-two million copies later (counting all eleven of the series published to date), the series still has at least three volumes to go, and every volume has had a protracted stay on the *New York Times* Best-sellers List.

Multnomah Press was next to score big successes with one of its authors. Bruce H. Wilkinson is an evangelist who noted the increasing popularity of self-help books of all kinds during the 1990s, but found most of the available offerings lacking in spiritual insight. He wrote a small book, *The Prayer of Jabez: Breaking through to the Blessed Life*, inspired by a brief passage in 1 Chronicles 4:10, which reads, "And Jabez called on the God of Israel, saying 'O that thou wouldest bless me indeed, and enlarge my coast, and that thine hand might be with me, and that thou wouldest keep me from evil, that it may not grieve me!' And God granted him that which he requested." The simple message of his book was that this was a prayer that God always answers. Multnomah published the volume in 2000, and it was an astonishing and nearly immediate success. At its peak, sales reached the million-book mark in a single month. Multnomah has built on the success of the original by bringing out related volumes yearly.

Miniature Editions, a subsidiary of Zondervan Publishing, scored its own major success with the 2003 publication of *The Purpose Driven Life* by evangelist Rick Warren. His book, intended as a guide for Christians undertaking a forty-day journey of spiritual discovery, was quickly taken up by churches across the country and across all Protestant denominations. Its adoption by church study groups boosted sales into the millions during its first year in print. More recently, the book has found a wider audience. In a widely reported hostage situation in 2005, it was purportedly instrumental in persuading the hostage-taker to release his captive and turn himself in to the authorities. The power of the message, read by the victim to her kidnapper, is said to have saved the day.

Modern Christian publishing is a huge and fast-expanding industry, having grown from $6.7 billion in 1994, just before the expansion into fiction and self-help, to $8 billion in 2004. And the established publishing houses represent only the tip of the iceberg. A dizzying array of houses that facilitate authors interested in self-publishing within the Christian framework have sprung up since the late 1990s. Maintaining industry-wide standards for Christian content and expression is the Christian Booksellers Association, with its 2,500 member stores, and the Evangelical Christian Publishing Association, to which most traditional and self-publishing Christian houses belong.

II

THE BIBLE AND BIBLICAL LITERATURE

The Christian literary tradition had its beginnings perhaps as early as 3,500 years ago. There are no originals of the original writings that became our earliest Old Testament books—it was not until those now-lost source documents were translated into Hebrew and Aramaic that copies were preserved. From archaeological digs and ancient libraries, we have inherited a vast number of documents, some whole and some in tantalizing scraps. Over the centuries, faith and its expression in inspired writings have gone hand in hand, as we have deepened our understanding of the Bible's message of hope and salvation.

Choosing the Canon

By approximately 200 B.C., all thirty-nine of the texts that make up the Old Testament, along with fourteen books of Apocrypha, had been written. By the end of the first century A.D., our familiar twenty-seven books of the New Testament had also been completed. Along with these texts, however, there were a great many other writings purporting to document the Word of God or the life of Jesus. It would take another 200 years before final agreement was reached as to which of these texts should be included in the biblical canon as directly inspired by God and which were the fallible products of mere historians and philosophers.

The oldest known Old Testament texts date to about 400 B.C. These are Hebrew and Aramaic translations of vastly more ancient original documents that no longer exist. Scholars believe, for example, that the original texts of the books of Genesis and Deuteronomy were first composed as early as 1400 B.C. The Dead Sea Scrolls, which contain the book of Isaiah and parts of all the other Old Testament books, were written much later, beginning in 200 B.C. In about 250 B.C., the first Greek translation of Old Testament texts appeared. This translation is called the *Septuagint* (Greek for "seventy") because it is thought to have resulted from the labor of seventy scribes and scholars.

Writings from and about the time of Christ's ministry on earth are more abundant and include many texts that do not appear in the modern Bible. These were written primarily in Greek, and more than 5,500 manuscripts have been found that tell the story of Christ or His ministry or claim to document the work of His apostles. Before A.D. 313 and the conversion of the Roman emperor Constantine to Christianity, there was no uniformity among Christian worshippers as to which texts were to be trusted as true accounts. Thus, there was a wide diversity in the way in which early Christians understood and professed their faith.

When the emperor Constantine made Christianity the state religion of Rome, Christians came out of their shadow existence as a persecuted sect, and it quickly became clear that the sometimes conflicting teachings of these many texts needed to be resolved. For the church to grow in strength and numbers, these internal contradictions had to be reconciled. Otherwise, there was a danger that the Christian movement would be broken apart into competing sects, fighting with one another over who was more accurately following the teachings of Christ.

Some of the disputed texts were quite radical. For instance, a church leader named Marcion, who offered one of the earliest compilations of New Testament texts (c. A.D. 140), rejected all the writings of Matthew, Mark, and John, as well as the book of Acts. He also rejected the Old

Testament in its entirety. He accepted as valid the epistles of Paul, but little else among the epistolatory writings of the New Testament we know today. He was motivated in these decisions by a desire to make a clean break from Judaism, and so he wished to eliminate all references to the Judaic past. Then again, Origen (185–254) accepted most of the writings that appear in our modern Bibles, but also wished to include the writings of Hermas, Barnabas, and Didache and disputed the validity of Paul's epistle to the Hebrews and the book of James.

By the late fourth century, the contentiousness among various sects within Christianity became too much for the bishop of Rome to bear. He commissioned a church scholar named Jerome to sift through all the competing and sometimes contradictory texts and to determine which ones should receive the approval, and authority, of the central church. Jerome completed his task in 384 (he was later named a saint for his efforts). The result of his labors is known as the *Vulgate Editio* (popular edition, commonly called the Vulgate), and it contained our familiar thirty-nine Old Testament texts and twenty-seven New Testament texts, along with fourteen additional books, called the Apocrypha.

The establishment of the biblical canon in the late fourth century did not end the textual controversies. Over the next 1,200 years, the Christian church was riven by dissension. This internal church controversy reached its apex with Martin Luther's challenge to the papacy. The pope convened the Council of Trent not only to deal with Luther's challenge but also to address a wide range of other problems facing the church. The council met over the course of nearly twenty years, from 1545 to 1563, and among its final decisions was the reaffirmation of the biblical canon established by Saint Jerome.

The Council of Trent was ineffective in stopping the Protestant movement, but the biblical canon it reaffirmed was adopted by the new churches of the Reformation. It was the Vulgate that was translated into English and then mass-produced through the new technology of the printing press. However, many Reformation leaders disputed the legitimacy of the Apocrypha, and chief among these dissenters was Luther.

Nonetheless, the Apocrypha continued to be translated and reproduced in nearly every Bible published before the 1800s. From Luther's time onward, however, they began to slip from their earlier position of prominence. By the time of the King James Version (1611), the books of the Apocrypha were relegated to an appendix and no longer appeared as a part of the primary text. By the 1880s, they were entirely omitted from Protestant Bibles and had been sidelined even in Catholic and Orthodox versions of the Holy Scripture. The biblical canon we know today was, at last, fully established.

In the latter part of the twentieth century, the world of biblical scholarship was periodically set abuzz by new linguistic theories and archaeological finds. The most important of the theories involved a hypothetical document called "Q" (for *quelle*, meaning "source"). This entirely theoretical document is imagined to have served as the original source for the writings of Matthew and Luke. Popular interest in "Q" has been based on claims that the similarities among the Gospels can only be explained by assuming that the writers employed the same sources. Detractors of the "Q" theory point out the obvious: If the disciples who wrote the Gospels both attended the same events in Christ's life, then they would naturally write of the incidents in similar terms. The archaeological discovery of the Dead Sea Scrolls, near the Middle Eastern town of Qumran (Israel), created another storm of controversy, mostly because the discoverers of the scrolls held such a tight monopoly of access to the documents. This touched off the inevitable conspiracy theories, which only began to be dissipated with the "unauthorized" publication of some scroll content. Thus far, the scrolls seem to validate the accepted biblical canon, rather than to challenge it.

History of the English-Language Bible

The earliest Bibles were relatively few in number. They were rendered in longhand by monastic scribes who wrote in Latin, which could be read only by the well-educated elites, principally officers of the church. The painstaking labor of producing Bibles by hand meant that each copy could take years of work to produce. Eventually, blocks of wood were carefully carved and used to print multiple copies of the Bible in a single printing, but this, too, was a laborious process, limiting the number of books that were produced. The common people were not permitted to read these Bibles, or even to own them—the punishment for owning one was execution. It would be another thousand years before everyday people could read the Word of God for themselves.

This occurred in the late 1300s, when certain reformers arose among the clergy, particularly in England, who were strongly opposed to the church's monopoly on the scriptures. One of these was John Wycliffe, who founded a reform movement called the Lollards and who enlisted his followers to reproduce dozens of copies of the Bible using the woodcut method. These volumes were then distributed to people outside the church hierarchy. His actions so angered the church that, forty years after his death, the pope ordered his bones be dug up and pulverized, then thrown into a river.

Wycliffe's Bibles, and those produced after his death by his follower, John Hus, were still produced in Latin, which meant that most people couldn't read the text. Their printing method, too, limited the production of the books. In 1455, however, a great invention set the stage for all this to change. That was the year when Johannes Gutenberg invented the printing press with moveable type. The very first book published with this new technology was the Bible, sometimes known as the forty-two-line Bible because there were forty-two lines of print on each page. For the first time, Bibles could be printed in large quantities, but still the church insisted that the common folk should not read it for themselves, and burned at the stake anyone caught possessing a private copy.

Meanwhile, reform-minded clergymen were growing increasingly upset by the Latin translation favored by the church, convinced that the authorized text contained grievous errors that contradicted Christian tradition. In 1476, the scholar John Colet put aside his Latin Bible and turned instead to the original Greek texts of the New Testament books. These he translated into English, producing a text that he felt was more rigorously faithful to the true gospel. He used this new text to teach his students at Oxford and read from it to throngs of London's residents from the steps of Saint Paul's Cathedral. Only his powerful friends kept him from execution by the church.

The first to combine the use of the English language with the high-volume capabilities of the printing press was William Tyndale. One of Wycliffe's admirers, Tyndale was exiled from then Catholic England for his beliefs. He traveled to Germany in 1525. There, he met with Martin Luther, who had just recently published the first German-language edition of the New Testament. With Luther's help, Tyndale completed the first press run of a mass-produced, English-language version in 1526. The church did not take kindly to Tyndale's actions and confiscated these Bibles almost as quickly as they could be run off on the printing press, but the movement to bring the Bible to the people could no longer be stopped.

Myles Coverdale, another English reformer, produced the first complete Bible translation, containing both the Old and New Testaments, in 1535. He was killed for his efforts, as was his colleague and friend, John Rogers, who did the actual printing of these books and was burned at the stake. Copies of the Bible that Rogers published were used as fuel for the fire that claimed his life. But in 1539, English reformers who wished to publish the Bible in the common language were finally safe from church persecution. In that year, King Henry VIII broke with the church, establishing the Church of England (Anglicans) in its place, and quickly authorized Bible publication in English. He even provided funding for the effort.

When Queen Mary took the English throne, she vowed to return

England to the Catholic Church, and Protestants of all sects were persecuted. Many fled into exile, and some traveled to Switzerland, where they worked to produce an English-language Bible that they could use in their homes. This work became known as the Geneva Bible, for the place where it was published, and it is the Bible that was brought to America by the Pilgrims and Puritans. It was the most popular version of the Bible, worldwide, until King James commissioned his version in 1611.

The King James Bible remained the most widely accepted English-language Bible for the next 200 years, although several attempts were made to replace it with new translations in both England and the Americas. The earliest American Bible was produced in 1663, but it was a translation of the King James Version into the Algonquin language. In 1833, Noah Webster tried his hand at a new translation, but even his fame (he had just previously published his extremely well-received dictionary) was not enough to challenge the primacy of the King James Version. It was only in the 1880s that a new translation, called the English Revised Version (ERV), effectively competed with the King James Version in popularity and sales. In America, the ERV was soon replaced by the American Standard Version (ASV), published in 1901, which was quickly adopted by most Christian churches.

Throughout the twentieth century, various new translations were offered to the public, each of them representing the effort of their publishers to bring the Bible's language closer to the language of everyday people. In 1971, a new edition of the ASV was produced, called the New

American Standard Version, and this was widely adopted by evangelicals and biblical scholars. It was acclaimed as the most accurate translation available at the time. But some critics faulted the translation method, saying that its reliance on a literal, word-for-word approach sacrificed the beauty and poetry of the original texts. An alternative version, the New International Version, attempted to remedy this problem, but many people were offended by the casual style it employed. Since the early 1970s, others have tried their hands at retranslation. In response to the drive toward political correctness of the 1980s and 1990s, the Today's New International Version was published in an attempt to eliminate all gender-specific language, but it was poorly received by most mainstream churches and their members. Most recently, translators have produced the English Standard Version, which attempts to preserve the accuracy of the American Standard Version, but does so in contemporary English.

Rare and Unusual Bibles

The history of Bible publishing is replete with extraordinary stories, many of which resulted in the existence of rare or unusual editions. From the Britches Bible of 1560 to the Judas Bible of 1602, many of these oddities are the result of typographical errors. Others, notably the first edition of the Tyndale Bible, can attribute their rarity to historical events.

The Tyndale Bible, first published in England in 1525–1526, owes its rarity to the church's adamant position that common people should not be allowed to read the Bible for themselves. In fact, the Catholic Church was probably Tyndale's best customer, because it sent its agents to buy up every copy they could find and then to destroy them before they could fall into the hands of the public. The agents were so thorough in their efforts that today only two copies of the first edition are known to survive.

The Britches Bible is another name for the Geneva Bible, which was published in 1560. This version was extremely popular in its time for several reasons. For instance, it was the first Bible edition to provide numbers for every verse. This was done because the Bible was intended for use in home study, and the numbering system made it so much easier to readily cite passages during lessons. The Britches Bible also provided extremely detailed margin notes and cross-references, again as an aid to self-study. Because of these special features, this version of the Bible was very popular among the Puritans and Pilgrims. But it derives its special name from something very different. In Genesis 3:7, when Adam and Eve suffer their fall from grace, they notice for the first time that they are naked and use fig leaves to cover themselves. Some translations of the Bible call these first bits of clothing *aprons*, others call them *loin cloths*, but the Geneva translators chose *breeches*, which is an archaic form of the slang term *britches*.

The Bishop's Bible was commissioned by the Anglican Church in direct response to the Geneva (Britches) Bible. The reason had nothing to do with britches, however. Of much greater concern was the commentary that was included in the margins, which was decidedly not respectful of the supremacy of the Anglican Church. Although very similar to the Geneva Bible in its translation of actual scripture, the Bishop's Bible replaced the margin notes with commentary more supportive of the Anglican Church hierarchy. The public, however, found the Geneva version much more to its liking, and the Bishop's Bible never gained a wide audience.

The first King James Version of the Bible was another attempt to challenge the popularity of the Geneva version. Early in his reign, King

James realized that the Bishop's Bible had been rejected by the public, and he sponsored the production of a whole new edition. Under his patronage, fifty scholars worked for six years to produce what they hoped would be the best, most accurate English translation of scripture ever published. Unfortunately, all their care and effort was compromised in several print runs, giving us the famous—or infamous—"He and She" Bibles. In certain printings, a typesetter seems to have fallen asleep on the job, because he allowed a typographical error to creep into the very end of Ruth 3:15, where it reads "he went into the city," when the correct phrase was "she went into the city." Only some of the Bibles printed in 1611 contained this error, and it was corrected by the end of that same year.

The Judas Bible and Vinegar Bible are, no doubt, similar examples of an inattentive typesetter. In the first case, published in 1609, the printer got confused while setting type. Intending to set the type for John 6:67 ("Then said Jesus unto the twelve, will ye also go away?"), the typesetter instead printed "Then said Judas unto the twelve." In the Vinegar Bible of 1717, the error appears in the heading that precedes Luke 20. There, the printer allowed "The Parable of the Vineyard" to become "The Parable of the Vinegar."

One error, however, was perhaps not so innocent. In 1631, the printer responsible for publishing the King James Bible was Robert Barker, who enjoyed the patronage of King Charles I. When the king placed a personal order for 1,000 copies of the Bible, it would have been wise to take extra care in proofreading the text. Unfortunately, all 1,000 copies suffered a glaring defect that went unnoticed until the books were delivered to the king. In Exodus 20:14, someone left out a crucial "not," so that the seventh commandment read, "Thou shalt commit adultery." Is it any wonder, then, that this version came to be known as the Wicked Bible?

America's Historic Bible

With the swearing in of every American president, we are reminded of the Christian tradition that underpins the founding of our nation. The new president is called on to take the oath of office, swearing to uphold his grave responsibilities with one hand on the Bible. Although each president is permitted to choose the Bible he will use in the ceremony, there is one that has a distinguished history and has been pressed into service by five presidents, beginning with George Washington.

In the pre-Revolutionary era, no Bibles were printed in the American colonies. Our historic Bible, a King James Version, was instead printed and bound in London in 1767 and brought to the colonies by Jonathan Hampton, a Freemason who belonged to the Saint John's Masonic Lodge in lower Manhattan. When Hampton was named grandmaster, he made a gift of the Bible to that Masonic lodge. This was an extraordinary gift. The handsome, leather-bound Bible was appointed with silver and was of great monetary value.

The Bible remained in the possession of the lodge for twenty years before it made its accidental entry into American political history. In the first years of American nationhood, New York City was the capital, and the first president was set to be sworn into office in front of Federal Hall. In the tumult and confusion of preparing for this momentous occasion, no one thought to secure a Bible on which Washington could swear his oath. At the last minute, New York's governor, Robert Livingston, remembered the Bible that graced the Saint John's Masonic Lodge nearby. Livingston had succeeded Hampton in the office of grandmaster. He offered Washington, a fellow Mason, the use of his lodge's Bible and quickly dispatched a runner to collect the valuable book. When the book was brought to the president, he opened it to Genesis 49–50, which tells of the death of Jacob and the mourning of his son, Joseph. When the inaugural ceremony was concluded, the Bible was returned to its accustomed resting place in New York. There it remained until Washington's death in 1799, when it was the Bible selected for scriptural reading at the first American president's funeral.

Other Masons rose to the presidency in the years following Washington, but until 1921 none elected to use the historic Bible. Warren G. Harding, however, chose to follow the precedent set by our first president. Whether he was motivated by a devotion to history or to his membership in the order is unknown. Dwight D. Eisenhower followed Harding's example in 1953, as did Jimmy Carter during his inauguration in 1977. The last to place his left hand on the aging maroon leather binding was George H. W. Bush in 1989. After his inaugural, the Bible remained on display in the nation's capital for another thirty days.

In 2001, George W. Bush fully intended to follow his father's example and take his oath of office on the Masonic Bible. Representatives of the Saint John's Masonic Lodge carefully packed up the precious volume and made the trip from New York's Pennsylvania Station to Washington, D.C. But the weather on that inaugural day conspired against even the best of plans. A torrent of rain was falling, and the participants in the inauguration huddled under umbrellas. The guardians of the Bible, possibly at the urging of Vice President—elect Dick Cheney, decided not to expose their precious cargo to the elements. Another Bible was quickly found to use in its place.

For years, the Masonic Bible rested in a place of honor at the Saint John's Masonic Lodge in New York, but in 1939 it was moved with great reverence to Federal Hall, which had been newly designated as a national museum, in recognition of that site's historic importance to our nation's early history. It has, however, sometimes been taken from its safe existence for display or use. It was the Bible from which scripture was read during the dedication ceremony for the Washington Monument in 1889. In 1965–1966, it was again brought into the public eye during the New York World's Fair. A national treasure, the Masonic Bible is under the care and protection of the National Parks Service.

Bible Concordances

A concordance is a reader's aide that offers a topically organized, alphabetically arranged index, with each entry followed by an exhaustive listing of all in-text references dealing with the subject at hand. This type of reader's guide permits the user to quickly locate a textual reference on any given subject. While concordances have been produced for all sorts of books, the Bible is particularly suited for such treatment, given its organization into numbered books, chapters, and verses.

The first true Bible concordance was created in the early 1200s by Saint Anthony of Padua, followed in 1263 by Hugh of Saint Cher's concordance of the (Latin) Vulgate Bible. Neither were intended for wide use, since the common people were prohibited from owning or reading the Bible at that time. These early concordances were clumsy, because no one had yet thought to number the individual verses (that would not happen until the publication of the Geneva Bible in 1560). But once the Bible began to be translated into contemporary languages (English and

German) and made available to the general public, the need for some kind of concordance became clear.

In 1722, the Scotsman Alexander Cruden began what would be a twelve-year obsession with the creation of a Bible concordance based on the King James Version. His concordance is an index of every significant word in the Bible, followed by an exhaustive list of every verse in which that word appears. Following its publication, *Cruden's Concordance* received both the approval of the king and the acceptance of the public. Throughout the centuries following its first publication, it has never been out of print.

While *Cruden's Concordance* is perhaps the best known, it does have shortcomings. *Cruden's* reliance on single-word index terms often meant that the user had to sift through dozens of entries before finding the verse that fit his or her needs. Later concordances would address this problem by basing the index on topical themes rather than specific, single words.

In the late 1800s, other biblical scholars took up the challenge handed down by Cruden. Orville J. Nave, a chaplain in the U.S. Army, compiled a topically oriented concordance in the late 1800s. The project took him twenty years and resulted in *Nave's Topical Bible*. He identified 20,000 topical themes, to which he associated a total of 100,000 scriptural references. At about the same time, James Strong, a scholar at the Drew Theological Seminary, began an even more ambitious project. Enlisting 100 like-minded colleagues, he compiled the classic *Strong's*

Exhaustive Concordance of the Bible, which first rolled off the presses in 1890. This concordance has had a profound influence on Bible study both among lay readers and in academic circles.

The rise of the electronic age has fostered a proliferation of online Bible concordances. The old classics can be found in electronic form, including *Cruden's, Nave's,* and *Strong's.* The Internet, however, allows for the expansion of these classic concordances' usefulness, because it permits the user to follow links to other Web sites where full-length articles on related scriptural topics can be found. A simple search using the phrase "Bible concordances" will bring the inquiring Bible student to a wealth of study guides and resources.

Book of Common Prayer

The *Book of Common Prayer*, first published in 1549, is the guiding text for worship within the Church of England and its overseas offshoot, the Episcopalian Church. It was suppressed at various times in its history and has undergone numerous revisions, but it has survived the four and a half centuries since its creation with its importance and influence intact.

The book owes its existence to England's King Henry VIII and his break with Catholicism when the pope refused to annul the king's marriage. He established the Church of England, with himself at its head, but otherwise did little to change the prayers, rituals, and modes of worship from those preferred by Rome. When his son, Edward VI, inherited the throne, he also inherited the office of head of the church and a national clergy that was strongly influenced by the Reform movement, particularly as expressed by Martin Luther and his followers.

Edward's bishops, who were under the leadership of Thomas Cranmer, the archbishop of Canterbury, were determined to make the liturgy of the Church of England less reflective of Catholicism, which they felt had strayed far from the teachings of Scripture. The bishops went through the received Catholic liturgy and stripped away all those elements that the Lutherans and other reformers deemed corrupt or contradicted by the Bible. In 1549, this new liturgical guide was published under the title the *Book of Common Prayer and Administration of the Sacraments and Other Rites and Ceremonies of the Church and after the Use of the Church of England.*

The word *common*, as it is used in the title, was chosen for two reasons. First, it reflected the decision of the bishops to adopt the common tongue, English, as the language of worship. Second, it reflected a law that was put into effect simultaneously with the publication of the book, the Act of Uniformity, which required that all churches share in common an identical approach to prayer, ritual, and other elements of worship.

The 1549 edition of the *Book of Common Prayer* was, in fact, four books in one. It contained a breviary, which is a list of approved daily prayers and the schedule according to which they must be said. It also contained a missal, which prescribed the appropriate conduct of the Mass, and a section called the pontifical, which set forth the appropriate prayers and conduct for high masses conducted by a bishop. Finally, there was the manual, to be used when performing occasional rituals, such as weddings and funerals.

The reformists of the time were not satisfied with the first edition of the *Book of Common Prayer*, believing that it preserved too many "popish" elements. They found an ally in Archbishop Cranmer, who was a strong admirer of Martin Luther's movement, and by 1552 a new and revised version was put forward. The new edition did away with many of the elaborate rituals that had been carried over from Catholicism and simplified both the churches and the garb of the clergy.

The new edition was much better received by both clergy and the general public, but it did not enjoy the support of Queen Mary, who followed Edward onto the throne six months after its publication. She was a devout Catholic, and among her first actions as queen was to reimpose her religion on the country and to suppress the *Book of Common Prayer*.

This situation lasted no longer than Queen Mary did, however. When Elizabeth I supplanted her on the throne in 1559, England was restored to Protestantism, and the *Book of Common Prayer*, in a slightly revised form, was reinstated as the authoritative text for worship in the Church of England.

The book underwent another, more substantial revision in 1662, during the reign of King James I (who also commissioned the King James Version of the Bible). This new edition raised dissension within the clergy, because many believed that it reintroduced far too many Catholic influences to the liturgy. These dissenters were known as the Puritans, and they broke with the Church of England to form their own sect.

Over the centuries, further revisions have been made to the text, and since the 1960s changes in the text have permitted worshippers a certain degree of latitude unheard of in earlier decades. It remains in wide use by Anglican and Episcopalian churches throughout the world.

Pilgrim's Progress

The year 1678 saw the publication of a remarkable book, *Pilgrim's Progress*. This book, written by John Bunyan, an itinerant Calvinist preacher, is an extraordinary allegorical tale of the path to redemption and was prized by devout Christians, particularly in the American colonies. For more than two centuries, it was likely to be found beside the Bible, and it was frequently used in the schools to teach children proper Christian values.

Bunyan was born in 1628 to a poor family in Bedfordshire, England. For the first part of his life, he struggled mightily to lead a pious life, but believed himself to have failed miserably. In about 1652 he made the acquaintance of Pastor John Gifford, who led a Protestant congregation that was independent of the dominant Church of England. He soon felt the call to preach, and by all reports he was very gifted. His knowledge of the Bible was exhaustive, and he could hold forth with great eloquence and scriptural authority on any spiritual subject. But to preach outside of the established Church of England was against the law.

In the early years of his preaching career, Bunyan came across the teachings of another independent religious sect, the Quakers. A firm believer in the Bible as the literal Word of God, Bunyan could not tolerate the Quaker way, which taught that each individual was bound to follow his or her own conscience in spiritual matters. Bunyan was moved to write a rebuttal of Quakerism, which was published in 1656. From that time on, he wrote constantly, producing a vast number of books over the course of the next thirty years.

Bunyan also continued to preach from whatever pulpit would have him, and in 1660 the authorities finally caught up with him. He was arrested in midsermon and consigned to jail. Although the court sentenced him to six months in prison, followed by exile from England, he was instead kept in his cell for the next twelve years. He continued to preach and write during this time and was finally released in 1672.

Free again, Bunyan was given permission to preach, and for the next few years his sermons drew ever greater crowds. But in 1675 the government once again began to crack down on "nonconformist" religious groups. Refusing to be silenced, Bunyan was arrested and imprisoned once again. In his jail cell, he found himself inspired to write a most ambitious work, an allegorical tale of inspiration and redemption that he would call *Pilgrim's Progress.* The book was published in 1678 and enjoyed immediate success with the public.

The pilgrim of the book's title is Christian, a young man of "deplorable condition" who is instructed by a character called Evangelist that he must make the journey from the "City of Destruction" to the "Celestial City," bearing a heavy pack containing all his sins. Along the way, Christian comes to the Cross, where his burden is miraculously eased. He passes through the Valleys of Humiliation and the Shadow of Death, the Slough of Despond, and the Dungeons of Doubting Castle, and he learns from characters named Discretion, Piety, Prudence, Chastity, Faithful, and Hopeful.

Bunyan's gift was his ability to use the everyday scenes and settings of rural life to illustrate the profound experience of spiritual redemption. His book became the model for all religious allegories that followed and remains widely read today. The allegory has inspired stage plays and song cycles as well and can be found on a variety of sites on the Internet. He died in London in 1688.

III

CARING AND SHARING

At the core of Christian values is the concept of charity, inherited from the laws of Moses and refined and clarified by the teachings of Jesus. In Deuteronomy 15:7, Moses exhorts us, "If there be among you a poor man . . . thou shalt not harden thine heart, nor shut thine hand from thy poor brother." This message is repeated in Christ's teachings. Both Matthew (19:21) and Mark (10:21) quote the Lord as saying, "If thou wilt be perfect, go and sell that thou hast, and give it to the poor, and thou shalt have treasure in Heaven; and follow me."

It is therefore no wonder that faith-based charitable organizations have long been a part of our tradition. Through these groups, from community soup kitchens to worldwide relief agencies, Christians endeavor to bring comfort to the suffering and assistance to the poor. The recent outpouring of support to the tsunami sufferers of Indonesia is just one manifestation of the spirit of Christian giving. That same spirit is at work every day, taking a vast array of forms. Learn, here, about just a small representative sampling of such groups and of the difficult, sometimes dangerous, and always inspirational work they do.

Boy Scouts

Most people do not think of the Boy Scouts as a charitable organization. They see it as little more than a wholesome, adult-supervised club for boys. But, from the days of its founding, the Boy Scouts has had a strong, charitable mission, both to the community that supports it and to the boys who join it.

The organization was founded in England by Robert Baden-Powell. He had served in the Boer War and drew on his experiences during that conflict to write a manual that could be used to train young men in a variety of skills while simultaneously instilling what he considered to be essential Christian values. In 1909, he published the manual *Scouting for Boys*, and it was an immediate success. Other organizations, including the Young Men's Christian Association and school-based groups, adopted the manual and formed groups. Within two years, the movement had spread to America and elsewhere around the world.

Because we are most familiar with the adventurous, outdoorsy aspect of scouting, it is easy to forget that this organization is not intended merely as a recreational option. The Boy Scouts of America (BSA) mission statement, however, clearly expresses the deeper values embodied by the group; "The BSA endeavors to develop American citizens who are physically, mentally, and emotionally fit; have a high degree of self-reliance. . . ; have personal values based on religious concepts; [and] have the desire and skills to help others."

The idea of service to others is explicitly stated in the scout slogan, "Do a good turn daily." Although membership is not restricted to Christians, the goal of the organization is to foster the development of Christian values in all its members. This is done through the merit badge program, in which all members must participate if they wish to move up through the scouting ranks. To earn a badge, a scout must demonstrate mastery in a particular area of endeavor, and mastery is proven not only by accomplishing a specific task (e.g., building a campfire or hiking) but by demonstrating strong personal growth as well.

There is a strong public service element to scouting. To qualify for many of the awards offered by the organization, a scout must earn badges in volunteer service besides the more recreationally oriented areas. This provides young boys the incentive to participate in, and learn the joys of, service to the less fortunate within their communities. Since 1992, the BSA has participated in National Youth Services Days, held in mid-April, encouraging its members to volunteer their time and efforts to projects ranging from soup kitchens and food banks to helping with adult literacy programs. The stress placed by scouting on traditional Christian values such as charitable giving and compassion explains why so many churches within the United States and around the world sponsor scout troops.

Christian Children's Fund

The Christian Children's Fund (CCF) was founded in 1938, when Dr. J. Calvitt Clarke, a Presbyterian minister, undertook a mission to China. There, he and his wife concentrated their efforts on helping war-orphaned children, who were suffering displacement and privation. To fund his efforts, Dr. Clarke formed the China Children's Fund and enlisted the support of U.S. churches back home. He spent the next thirty-five years at this labor, eventually expanding his work to include poor and orphaned children throughout Asia. Today, the CCF serves thirty-two countries around the world. Along the way, the name of the organization was changed to reflect its expanded territorial reach.

Anyone familiar with late-night television has heard of the CCF and its basic appeal for sponsors. Individuals are invited to "adopt" a child for a small monthly donation. In return, the donor receives letters from the adopted child or from the child's caregivers and is kept updated on the child's progress. This system has been very successful, because it puts a human face on the need that is being addressed. Donations are used to provide health and educational facilities, to cover the cost of food and medical care, and to improve living conditions in regions where clean water and safe housing are hard to come by.

The success of the CCF is also due to a rigorous commitment to accountability. The organization commits nearly 81 percent of each donation to actual relief efforts, retaining far less than most other groups to cover administration costs. But the CCF doesn't stop there. It also closely monitors the actual disposition of the charitable funds to make certain that they are being used in the most appropriate and effective way. Too often, relief agencies simply hand over funds to local agencies and then lose track of how the money is spent.

By 2004, the CCF had expanded greatly in both scope and funding. More than $138 million was made available to fund projects that directly benefit more than 7.6 million of the world's poorest children. It is highly respected among the world's relief-oriented fund-raising agencies because of its commitment to its mission, the integrity of its administration, and the practical successes achieved by the projects it funds.

Church World Service

At the end of World War II, an exhausted Europe was faced with what looked like an impossible task of rebuilding. Farms and industries were devastated, leaving millions of people without work, and the destruction that rained down on towns and cities left behind a huge homeless population as well. The governments of Europe could not begin to address the problem, nor could any single organization at the time hope to provide anything more than token assistance.

Recognizing the scope of the problem, a number of church leaders representing a broad range of Christian denominations decided to join together and pool their resources. Recognizing that no individual church group could hope to succeed alone, they reached out to one another to create a thirty-six-denomination coalition. Their mission was simple and derived directly from the teachings of Jesus: "Feed the hungry, clothe the naked, heal the sick, comfort the aged, shelter the homeless." Before the year was out, the Church World Service (CWS) had sent millions of tons of supplies to Europe's needy and had made a significant contribution to easing the huge refugee problem by sponsoring the resettlement of people who had been displaced during the war.

Once the worst of Europe's crisis had been addressed, the CWS turned its attention to the rest of the world. Its Immigration and Refugee Program still sponsors the relocation and resettlement of refugees fleeing war or political oppression. The CWS also formed the Christian Rural Overseas Program to organize the fight against world hunger. It appealed to churches throughout the country to collect food donations, which were then shipped out to help feed the poor of Europe, Asia, Latin America, and Africa.

Today, the CWS combines the direct provision of aid to the needy with a more far-seeing policy of underwriting development programs that will pay long-term dividends for the poor and providing volunteer labor to carry the projects to completion. CWS funds and volunteers have participated in a soil-erosion project in Algeria and drought-relief efforts in India, among many other long-term programs.

But the CWS remains best known for its work as a disaster-relief agency. Contributions of time, money, food, and blankets have eased suffering throughout the world. During the worst years of the Sahelian drought, aid was given to Sudan, Somalia, and other affected countries. After Nicaragua and Guatemala were struck by devastating earthquakes in the 1970s, CWS volunteers were among the first to help in the rebuilding efforts. More recently, the CWS has provided relief to the war-torn Balkans and to Indonesia's tsunami-devastated peoples.

Gideons International

In 1898, two traveling men, strangers to one another at the time, chanced to register for rooms in a Wisconsin hotel where, due to an unusually large number of guests, they were asked to share accommodations. The men, John H. Nicholson and Samuel E. Hill, agreed to the suggestion rather than take their chances that rooms would be available elsewhere in the town. That evening, while readying himself for bed, Nicholson took out his Bible, from which he customarily read before going to sleep. Hill noticed, and shared with Nicholson the fact that he, too, was a Christian. The two shared fellowship that night, and during this chance meeting the seeds of what would become an extraordinary evangelical movement were sown.

When their hotel stay was ended, the two men promised to keep in touch with one another, and in the following year they got together with Will J. Knights, a third man who also understood the loneliness of the solitary Christian traveler. At this meeting, held in a Young Men's Christian Association in Nicholson's hometown of Janesville, Wisconsin, they formed the nucleus of an organization dedicated to helping Christian travelers find fellowship on the road. The goal was to foster spiritual growth, encourage service to the Lord, and spread the Word of the Gospels. It was Knights who came up with the name of the organization, drawing on the sixth and seventh chapters of the book of Judges for his inspiration. Knights argued that members of this fledgling evangelical society should model themselves after Gideon, whose humility, devotion, and obedience to the Word of God was absolute and completely selfless.

While the Gideon Society was initially formed to provide a network of Christian support and fellowship for Christian men who were forced by their work to spend much of their lives on the road, the founders wanted to include in their organization a formal evangelical mission. They found it difficult to come up with a practical means by which to achieve this goal, however, and for the first seven years of the organization's existence, its founders simply recruited new members one by one as they encountered other Christian travelers during their business trips.

In 1907, however, the group held a meeting in Chicago at which they considered other evangelical options. One of the conference attendees suggested that the group collect funds to purchase a supply of Bibles. Members would carry these with them on their business trips and leave one behind at the reception desk of every hotel at which they stayed. This way they could ensure that every other Christian traveler would always be able to find a Bible to turn to for inspiration, even though he was far from home. In 1908, this modest plan was greatly expanded when a member suggested that the association take their activities plan much further. Rather than leave but a single copy at each hotel, the idea was to leave a copy in every room. This practice would serve the society's aims in three ways: by offering inspiration to the weary Christian traveler, by offering mute but powerful testimony to non-Christians who might be brought to Jesus, and by providing a way to enlist new members.

The society quickly agreed to this plan, which was to be funded through donations from its members. However, a pair of Christian men who were familiar with the Gideon mission soon came up with the means to greatly expedite the plan. These men, Frank Garlick and A. B. T. Moor, were active in the Ministerial Union, which served to unite a variety of Protestant denominations on a large number of issues. They carried the word of the Gideons to that organization, with the suggestion that the union provide support. Garlick's pastor, Dr. E. R. Burkhalter, led the union in that decision. Calculations as to the annual cost of the enterprise were made, and the union's member churches were each asked to contribute to the cause in accordance with the size of their congregations.

While most of us are familiar with the Gideons because of the Bibles it places in hotels, the association has added to its mission over the years. It now places Bibles in every place where they might serve the spiritual needs of the lonely or the desperate, including hospitals, prisons, and homeless shelters. In World War II, it began the practice of distributing Bibles to members of the military, and in later decades it also offered free Bibles to students in primary and secondary schools, as well as in colleges and universities.

From a small, Wisconsin-based men's association, the Gideons organization has expanded to become truly international. Chapters have formed in 179 countries, and the Bibles it distributes have been translated into 82 languages. It distributes more than 52 million Bibles every year and regularly returns to hotels and other distribution areas to replace copies that have been taken away. The church-based support it receives continues to be generous, but as the society's mission has expanded it has also turned to the broader community for donations.

Lutheran World Relief

One of the largest disaster and emergency relief organizations in existence, the Lutheran World Relief (LWR) got its start during the years immediately following World War II and participated in the broad affiliation of Christian church groups that formed the Christian World Service. Created by the Lutheran Church–Missouri Synod, the LWR now focuses all its efforts on providing supplies and reconstruction assistance following disasters around the globe. Equally important to its mission is its long-term goal of individual empowerment. It supports programs that will provide "lasting solutions to poverty and injustice."

In Africa, the LWR is active in ongoing rural development projects as well as in the fight against AIDS/HIV. In Asia and the Middle East, it is involved in advocacy for political, social, and economic rights for people traditionally excluded from power. It is a stong advocate for women's rights to participate in public life. It is also engaged in efforts to improve the provision of basic needs, particularly water supplies in drought-plagued regions, and in environmental protection. In Latin America, the LWR's efforts have improved access to land for the rural poor, disaster relief and prevention, and conflict resolution.

Compared to other charitable agencies, the LWR has an enviable record of efficiency and accountability. It survives on donations, and a full 90 percent of all monies received is spent directly on relief and advocacy efforts, retaining only 10 percent to cover administrative costs. (In the field of charitable giving, the average proportion of donated funds devoted to administrative and other nonrelief purposes is closer to 20 percent.)

The LWR does not use its relief efforts as a proselytizing mission among the needy it attempts to serve. It does, however, solicit more than mere money from its donors. Along with financial contributions, it encourages donors to offer prayers for the needy, recognizing the importance of spiritual support, even when offered from afar.

Missionary Societies

The Christian missionary tradition begins with the ministry of Jesus Himself, who went forth among the people to deliver the word of salvation. It is in emulation of His work that Christians have, ever since, considered it a fundamental duty to share and spread the Word of Christ throughout the world. Often combining humanitarian works with the teaching of the Word, missionaries have brought Christianity to every corner of the world, but they could not have achieved such success were it not for the missionary societies that provided (and still provide) them with financial support and spiritual guidance.

Nearly all early Christians understood that a fundamental part of their worship was to witness to others the message left behind by Jesus, and the rapid growth of the church even during the first 300 years of persecution is a testament to their diligence and devotion. In later years, the Church of Rome established special monastic orders dedicated to this mission, the most famous of which were the Jesuits. During the Protestant Reformation era, the newly formed Christian denominations depended on evangelizing not only for the spiritual purpose of saving souls but also to increase their ranks.

By the 1700s, nearly every Christian denomination supported an evangelical or missionary effort, whether through local outreach programs or through missionaries sent abroad. Only a few, primarily utopian religious settlements contented themselves with "natural recruitment" over the generations and held themselves apart from the outside world. By the 1800s, Protestant missionary societies had become widespread. Some were affiliated with a single denomination, such as the Anglican Society for the Propagation of Christian Knowledge and the American Baptist Foreign Mission Society. Others were somewhat more ecumenical in nature, such as the predominantly but not exclusively Congregationalist organization known as the London Missionary Society.

The work of foreign missions is threefold: to inspire conversion by local inhabitants through preaching the Gospels, to offer by example a glimpse of the blessings of Christian life, and to plant new churches in communities where none had previously existed. Missionaries traveling to foreign lands often face conditions of extreme hardship and even threats to their lives, but are drawn to this service by the strength of their faith and their desire to carry out the Lord's work. They live among the people to whom they minister, sharing in both the joys and sufferings of the local community. Through their efforts, Christianity has been spread throughout the world.

But the missionary spirit is not restricted to service in exotic lands. Denominationally specific missions are carried out here at home as well. Some denominations are well-known for their requirement that every adult member participate in missionary work. For instance, the Church of Jesus Christ of Latter Day Saints, familiarly known as the Mormons, has such a requirement, as does the Jehovah's Witness movement. They can be found in every community, knocking on doors and offering to share their understanding of the Bible to all who will listen. Most missionaries, however, take up this form of service because they have felt a very personal, individual call to carry the message of Jesus out into the world.

Order of the Eastern Star

The Order of the Eastern Star (OES) is a charitable organization affiliated with the the Fraternal Order of Freemasons. (Freemasonry, once closely associated with the Crusades and the Catholic Church, was disavowed by the papacy in 1738, but several Protestant denominations still embrace it and its fraternal and benevolent goals.) The order was first conceived by Dr. Rob Morris, a prominent Mason and lifelong educator, while he was teaching at a private school in Oxford, Mississippi. He felt that women should be able to share in the opportunity for growth and spirituality that men gained through their involvement with Masonry. Working with his wife, Charlotte, and later with the assistance of other like-minded Masons and their wives, he developed the plan for the Order of the Eastern Star.

In 1855, the first chapter of the order was convened in New York, to which Morris and his wife had moved from Mississippi. This chapter issued charters to Masonic temples throughout the United States that expressed an interest in forming their own OES chapters. By 1876, OES chapters had been formed in thirteen states. Today, there are 8,000 chapters worldwide, and a total membership of approximately 1 million men and women. The organization publishes a magazine for its membership, *The Eastern Star Journal*, which features articles about the variety of public-service projects and charitable drives being undertaken by member groups.

The OES draws on the Bible for its inspiration and considers the spiritual development of its members to be paramount. However, it stresses that spiritual development is best wed to charitable service. Its member chapters are free to choose the causes to which they will lend support. In recent years, OES chapters have raised funds for research into the treatment and cure of Alzheimer's disease, juvenile asthma, and juvenile diabetes. The order also offers scholarships to young people who wish to pursue a degree in theology. Many of the order's projects focus on healthcare and the care of the elderly.

While open to individuals from a wide range of Christian denominations, membership is restricted to Masons or their adult family members. As with the Masonic tradition to which they are attached, meetings are imbued with a great deal of biblically derived ritual, but the details of these rituals are held in confidence by members. This has perpetuated an aura of mystery about Masonry and the OES that has given rise to a great many faniciful notions. In fact, however, the OES is wholly dedicated to fostering Christian fellowship and to an ethic of public service among its members.

Promise Keepers

Traditionally, the athlete epitomized a great many positive virtues: self-discipline, talent, strength of body and of character, honor, and integrity. Little wonder, then, that sports figures were among the people most frequently named as "heroes" or "role models." When people spoke of "sportsmanship," they implied grace under pressure and decent living. But by the late twentieth century, the cult of high-paid "sports celebrities" seemed to have driven all these positive values from the scene. Meanwhile, in the broader culture it seemed as if the ideas of responsibility and maturity had become unfashionable. Divorce rates were soaring, family obligations went unmet, and attendance at church services was falling to an all-time low.

In 1990, however, two young athletes decided to do what they could to reverse this trend. Dave Wardell and Bill McCartney, both affiliated with the University of Colorado, had never lost sight of their Christian faith. On their way to attend a banquet hosted by the Fellowship of Christian Athletes, they got into a discussion of the best ways to help promote spiritual and emotional maturity among their fellow athletes and among men in general. With this conversation, the organization known as Promise Keepers was born.

McCartney and Wardell were convinced that the answer to the modern malaise was to be found in Christian revival and in inspiring discipleship in America's young men. They agreed that the best way to achieve both was by sponsoring large-scale inspirational meetings, to which as many as 50,000 young Christian men would be called to prayer. They sought the assistance of Chuck Lane, then deeply involved in the Christian outreach group called Campus Crusade. They then recruited among their own circle of friends and associates, bringing together a total of seventy-two individuals who were committed to making McCartney and Wardell's vision a reality.

The first revival and prayer meeting was held in July 1991 on the University of Colorado campus and was attended by 4,200 men. Although smaller in scale than McCartney's grand vision, it was a solid beginning. At the end of the event, the 4,200 were asked to commit to attending another meeting in 1992, and each was asked to bring twelve new recruits with him.

In the year that followed, Promise Keepers refined its organization and mission. First it organized a team to solicit the support of churches throughout the state. Through this outreach, it came to the attention of Dr. James Dobson, whose inspirational radio show was heard throughout the country. When he made mention of the Colorado-based group,

Promise Keepers began receiving inquiries from churches in every state of the Union.

The theme of the second Promise Keepers conference was interdenominational and interracial reconciliation. Attendance exceeded 24,000, and the young men came from all over the country. Between conferences, the core organizers also hosted a leadership conference, at which pastors from churches across the country were invited to contribute to the development of the organization's goals. In 1993, McCartney's dream of convening 50,000 men in Christian fellowship was achieved. Now it was necessary for the group to expand from the University of Colorado campus, and in succeeding years simultaneous events were held at campuses around the country.

The name "Promise Keepers" derives from a series of promises to which each member commits. These promises include a commitment to honor Jesus Christ, physical and spiritual purity, fulfilling civic and familial responsibilities, and community service. In keeping these promises, members also commit to honoring the Ten Commandments in all aspects of their lives. By 2004, attendance at Promise Keepers conferences had grown to 200,000, and the movement continues to expand.

Promise Keepers is not without controversy within the Christian community. Some of the more fundamentalist churches take issue with the organization's broad ecumenicalism, particularly its willingness to welcome Catholics to their annual conferences. In addition, some groups have raised objections to what is perceived as a too-humanistic understanding of psychology and say that the organization's printed materials stray from a literal reading of Scripture. Nonetheless, Promise Keepers has received a warm reception across a broad spectrum of denominations and has been praised for its efforts in revitalizing Christian values among the young men to whom it sends out its call.

Red Cross

In 1859, the Swiss businessman Henri Dunant was traveling to meet with the French emperor Napoléon III to secure water rights for one of his investment deals. His journey took him to the Italian town of Solferino, from which Napoléon was conducting a war with Austria. Dunant arrived in time to witness the aftermath of a terrible battle and was sickened by the sight of so many wounded needing care but receiving none. He wrote of the carnage, and in his book *A Memory of Solferino* (1862) he offered suggestions as to how such suffering might be avoided in the future.

His ideas were taken up by the Geneva Public Welfare Society, in Switzerland, which formed an agency dedicated to providing nonpartisan protection and assistance to soldiers wounded in war. In 1863, a conference was called to make this vision a reality, and representatives of sixteen European countries attended. At this conference, each participating nation was invited to create a body of volunteers who would carry out the larger organization's principles of wartime care for the sick and injured. Thus was the International Red Cross born. Twelve U.S. states immediately committed to the project, with the remainder joining a few years later. The United States was not a participant in this first conference, but formed its own Red Cross Society in 1881 nonetheless, under the leadership of Clara Barton.

During the early decades of its existence, the Red Cross dedicated its efforts strictly to easing wartime suffering, but quickly expanded its assistance to include helping the citizens of war zones as well as aiding the soldiers. Crucial to its success was its reputation for maintaining strict neutrality—Red Cross volunteers did not take sides in any conflict. Because of this neutrality, Red Cross vehicles were permitted passage, unmolested, through the thick of battle to carry out their mission of healing.

The Red Cross societies of the individual nations, including the American Red Cross, are largely autonomous, although they take guidance regarding general policies and practices from international headquarters in Geneva. Over the years, the mission of the Red Cross has grown. In addition to helping those wounded in wartime, it added humanitarian relief to disaster areas around the world. The American Red Cross also devotes time and resources to helping veterans of the military and to public health initiatives. It established a nationwide program of collecting and distributing blood and blood products to healthcare facilities throughout the country, particularly in response to extraordinary demand due to natural or man-made disasters. The organization also sponsors readiness training programs, such as first aid and lifesaving classes through the public schools and agencies such as the Young Men's and Young Women's Christian Associations.

The Red Cross is not associated with any particular Christian denomination. Nonetheless, its familiar cross-shaped logo implies the Christian values that underlay the organization's goals and mission. It does not evangelize, but expresses the teachings of Jesus through the actions of its members, no matter their individual religious affiliation. Regardless of its nondenominational character, it is strongly associated with Christianity—so much so that Muslim nations have chosen to form their own organization (the Red Crescent) rather than affiliate themselves with the Red Cross movement.

Salvation Army

In 1861, the Methodist minister William Booth began his evangelical work among the poor of London. His work was twofold: to spread the Gospels and to provide comfort and charity to the needy. He was soon joined in his work by his wife, Catherine, and together they began their plans to carry out their work on a much grander scale. In 1865, Booth began holding revivals around the London area, and at first called his new movement the East London Revival Society, but quickly changed the name to the Christian Mission. He proved an effective speaker, and soon crowds were thronging to his revival tents.

In 1878, Booth decided that, just as he had increased the scope of his preaching, so, too, should he expand the social welfare work that was always a part of his mission. He and his wife borrowed the organizational style of the British army and designed uniforms to continue the military theme, the better to symbolize their intent to "wage war on evil." They renamed their ministry the Salvation Army and established soup kitchens where all the poor were welcome, but laid down strict ground rules for entry: No drink was allowed, for instance, and all who partook of the offered meals were expected to listen to Booth's sermons. This way, the minister reasoned, he could provide sustenance for the soul as well as the body.

No doubt some who came to the soup kitchens turned a deaf ear to the religious message, but the Booths attracted many converts through their good works. From these converts, they recruited their army, which they sent forth to solicit donations to fund further projects, such as shelters for the indigent and the distribution of warm clothing and blankets. In 1880, George Railton, a high-ranking member of the army, brought a team of seven women to Pennsylvania to found the first Salvation Army outpost in the United States. Once the movement began to spread in the United States, Booth's daughter, Evangeline, was sent over to take charge of the American operations. In 1890, the movement had grown so much that Booth composed a manual of standard practices, principles, and procedures, *In Darkest England and the Way Out*. In 1926, the organization expanded and refined these doctrines in the official *Handbook of Salvation Army Doctrine*.

In the years since the Booths opened their first soup kitchen, the Salvation Army has grown tremendously. It now has branches in 100 countries and serves the spiritual and temporal needs of millions. Actual membership in the army exceeds 3 million. Leadership positions are given to members who have attended Salvation Army schools. These officers run facilities that range from maternity homes to job training centers, from orphanages to alcohol rehabilitation units. While charitable donations contribute an important part of the army's funding, some of the facilities it operates provide additional sources of revenues, such as the residences it maintains in New York and other large cities for retirees and young working women.

Although the Salvation Army wages spiritual war against poverty and evil, it is no stranger to the profane conflicts of the secular world. During the twentieth century's two world wars, Salvation Army volunteers headed to the battlefronts, bringing services to the soldiers through their mobile canteens. Since then, the Salvation Army has always sent support and supplies to its counterparts in the national military. In addition, the Salvation Army has historically been among the first of the major charitable organizations to send assistance to the victims of natural disasters around the world. Perhaps the best known of the Salvation Army's activities is the annual Christmas charitable appeal, when bell ringers can be found on nearly every street corner beside the familiar Salvation Army kettle, mutely soliciting donations from passers-by.

By 1934, the Salvation Army had grown to a truly international effort, with branches in nearly every major European country. The international operation is overseen from offices in London. To keep members informed and to provide a venue for public outreach, the army publishes the weekly magazine *War Cry*.

Sojourners

The Sojourners are members of a faith-based community that draws its members from a broad spectrum of Christians and are dedicated to bringing the inspiration of faith into public life. Since their inception in 1971, they have devoted their efforts toward bearing public witness to Jesus while working to improve the lives of the most vulnerable of His children.

The organization was founded by Jim Wallis, while he was a student at Trinity Evangelical Divinity School in Deerfield, Illinois. He had grown up in a privileged Detroit, Michigan, family during the 1960s and had witnessed firsthand the great inequalities between the well-to-do of his family's social circle and the poor, predominantly African American inhabitants of that city's slum neighborhoods. While still an undergraduate, studying at Michigan State University in the latter half of the 1960s, he organized a number of his classmates into discussion groups to explore the issues of race, class, and war.

During this period, Wallis found it difficult to reconcile the

Christian faith of his upbringing with the suffering he saw all around him. This crisis of faith, not uncommon for young people of conscience, caused him to temporarily turn from the church. As he neared the end of his undergraduate years, however, he began to understand that only a spiritual renewal could bring about the profound changes that he felt were needed in the world. Thus inspired, he enrolled in seminary studies at Trinity Evangelical Divinity School.

Here, Wallis found that he was not alone in his desire to combine spiritual values with public works. With several like-minded seminary students, he founded a faith community called the Sojourners' Fellowship, which took its name from Hebrews 11:8–10. In time, the group decided to create a publication that would spread the word of their work and faith. This newsletter, the *Post-American*, eventually became today's *Sojourner's Magazine*.

The first group of Sojourners established a communal home in a poor neighborhood in Deerborn, and soon other communities sprang up in similar areas near other campuses around the country. These communities worshipped together, but also looked outward, offering volunteer services to the people of their neighborhoods, primarily by providing after-school and summer education programs for the local children. In 1975, members of the original group moved to Washington, D.C., and settled in Columbia Heights, then a desperately poor, predominantly African American neighborhood. There, they set up school programs and soup kitchens and engaged in an active youth ministry.

Central to the Sojourner mission is a profound faith in the power of compassion, community, and commitment. The original communal model of the early Sojourner households eventually fell away, but the deep involvement in local and national public life remains strong. Wallis reached out across denominational lines to enlist a broad range of Christian churches and faith-based organizations into the mission of service that the Sojourners espouse, hoping to break down the barriers of political partisanship that so often interfere with attempts at social progress.

Volunteers of America

Ballington Mumford Booth was the son of William Booth, the founder of the Salvation Army. Ballington joined his father's ministry at an early age and in 1885 was sent to Australia to lead the formation of a branch of the army. After successfully completing this mission in 1887, Ballington was next sent to the United States, where he took charge of the American branch of the organization with the help of his wife, Maud. In 1896, however, Ballington and Maud withdrew from the army, having come to disagree with some of its policies. Still devoted to Christian service and to spreading the gospel, they created their own charitable organization, Volunteers of America.

The Booths began their work in urban centers, setting up operations in the poorest districts and offering a variety of social services, including the first rehabilitation centers (halfway houses) for men newly released from prison. By the 1920s, their organization had given birth to numerous day nurseries, low-rent residences for the homeless, and summer camps and was firmly established among the faith-based charitable organizations of the day.

In 1930, however, their resources and resilience were put to a real test. This was the dawn of the Great Depression, when so many people were thrown out of work that the nation's social welfare system was strained beyond the breaking point. Volunteers of America responded to the crisis by expanding its organization and adding new programs to its menu of services. It offered everything from job training and placement services to food distribution centers.

Like the Salvation Army, Volunteers of America has always provided support for the nation's military efforts. It has sponsored and staffed battlefront canteens, and during World War II it launched a series of "salvage drives" to collect scrap rubber and metal for reuse in the war effort.

Among the greatest successes scored by Volunteers of America has been the organization's involvement in creating affordable housing for the poor and low-income workers. The group worked in partnership with the federal government and twenty-eight state governments to build low-cost housing projects during the 1960s and 1970s. It has also led in the development of affordable nursing care for the elderly and the chronically ill. With a professional staff of 14,000, aided by a volunteer base numbering 70,000, the organization estimates that it provides its services to 1.8 million of America's needy every year.

YMCA/YWCA

The Young Men's Christian Association (YMCA) and the Young Women's Christian Association (YWCA) today serve 120 countries around the world and provide services to 45 million people annually. In the United States, there are more than 2,500 association chapters, serving 10,000 local communities and boasting a membership of 17.9 million men, women, and children.

The first of the two organizations to form was the YMCA, which was founded in London in 1844. At that time, the major cities were facing an unprecedented influx of young men from the countryside in search of work. The Industrial Revolution had severely reduced the ability of the agricultural sector to provide jobs on the nation's farms, and young men were drawn to factory employment and other newly invented city-based jobs.

The cities simply could not accommodate this flood of new inhabitants. Some of the young men were permitted to live in their workplaces, but most were forced to make do with whatever shelter they could find. In London, street life had grown dire, as muggings and assaults occurred with frightening regularity. One of the young rural men borne along on this tide of city-bound job seekers was George Williams. He had no trouble finding work and shelter, but was not blind to the situation in the streets around him. In 1841, he got together with a handful of other young Christian men to form a residential Bible study group, and they called their organization the Young Men's Christian Association.

The idea caught on slowly but steadily. Ten years after that first group's inaugural meeting, twenty-three others had sprung up in urban areas throughout England. Membership had grown from a handful of Bible students to a nationwide total of 2,700. And in that same year, 1851, the idea went international, with the establishment of the first YMCA chapters in the United States and Canada. One year later, the first YWCA was formed along the model of the men's organization. Two years later, the YMCA boasted chapters in seven countries and a total membership exceeding 30,000.

The YMCAs and YWCAs offered single young men and women a wholesome residential alternative to the dangers and temptations of life lived closer to the streets. The cost of staying in a chapter residence was minimal, but there were rules of behavior that had to be followed; in particular, the use of alcohol was banned. With rules of residence and a dedication to Bible study, the associations soon developed the reputation of being islands of peace in the otherwise tumultuous life of the cities.

Over the years, the activities sponsored by the YMCA expanded beyond Bible study to include physical training and lecture programs, the better to develop young men's physical and intellectual lives along with nurturing their spiritual development. Residences were built in dormitory style, with shared bathrooms. Income from room rents provided the bulk of the association's funding up through the 1980s.

The American YMCA movement stumbled during the Great Depression, when joblessness was so great that few men could afford even the minimal rents charged in the residences. The association responded by expanding its mission, creating or renewing partnerships with local churches and community groups. The YMCAs opened their doors to the public, offering gym membership and lecture series in an effort to raise additional funding. They weathered the storm, but faced a new challenge during World War II.

With so many men drafted to serve the war effort, several YMCAs found themselves with too many vacancies to remain financially viable. At the same time, an unprecedented number of women were entering the workforce. Many residences chose to offer housing to women. At the end of the war, returning soldiers were choosing to live in the newly created suburbs rather than in the cities, and many of the old urban residences were allowed to close down, while new buildings were going up elsewhere. New programs, including child care for working mothers, were introduced as the need made itself known during the 1960s and 1970s. In the 1980s, with the explosion of the fitness craze, YMCAs saw a resurgence in revenues from gym memberships.

One fatality of the trends of recent decades, however, was a key service that the original associations were formed to provide. While YMCAs still offer a wide variety of services, the residential program is no longer available in most parts of the country, and most rooming facilities are devoted to short-term stays for travelers.

IV

CHRISTIANITY AND THE AMERICAN EXPERIENCE

Christianity is a worldwide religion and had its beginnings in the region we now call the Middle East. But it has played a special role in the foundation and development of the United States, a role unparalleled in any other nation of the world. The first American colonies were founded by Christians fleeing religious persecution in England, and the principles and values they brought with them to this New World found expression in the terms according to which the nation was formed.

While it is true that America has always opened its doors to a wide variety of cultures, ethnicities, and religious traditions, it is nonetheless true that the nation's fundamental documents and principles derive from the predominantly Protestant communities that descended from the early colonial settlements. To explore the depth of this Christian influence, we need only to look at the early colonial settlements, at the documents on which our society is based, and at the traditions that are so closely associated with what it means to be "an American."

Pilgrims and Puritans

The early colonists who settled America's eastern shores were of two distinct groups, both of whom were in conflict with the established Church of England. One group was called the Separatists, also called the Pilgrims. This tiny Protestant sect derived its name from the belief that the Church of England was so corrupt and deviant from Scripture that there was no alternative—for the sake of their souls they had to separate themselves from it completely. The Puritans, the other group, adopted a less drastic point of view. They agreed with the Separatists that the Church of England was in error on any number of scriptural and procedural points. However, they chose to retain some semblance of an association with the state church, while purging their own services of what they considered to be false doctrine or erroneous practice. They felt that, by their example, they could help lead the Church of England back to a more pure, doctrinally correct form of worship.

Since the Church of England imposed its doctrine and practice on all the nation's congregations, it was no surprise that the Separatists could not long abide in England. A Separatist congregation in Nottingham finally could no longer tolerate the persecution it received from the established church and agents of the king. The first émigrés set sail for Amsterdam, but life in Holland was very hard. In time, they decided to leave Europe entirely and take their chances at creating a whole new community of faith in the New World. One hundred and two men, women, and children, many of whom were members of the Separatist sect, boarded the *Mayflower* in the summer of 1620 for the Atlantic crossing and arrived at Plymouth Rock, on what is now the Massachusetts coast, in the winter of that same year.

The Pilgrim colony at Plymouth was led by William Bradford, who hoped to establish a truly perfect human society based on the precepts of the Bible. He established a government based on direct participation by all freemen of the colony. This idea, of citizen self-government rather than rule by a king, was very new and remained an important inspiration in the colonies up to the time of the American Revolution. However, there is no way of knowing how successfully the Plymouth colonial government might have been, because most of the settlers died in the first year, and the survivors were forced to take refuge in neighboring colonies, most of which were founded by Puritan groups.

The Puritans had been under far less pressure to leave England, at least at first. They were far more numerous than the Separatists, and many Puritans were of the noble classes and held positions of public trust. However, British church and political history of the period was extremely volatile. During the English Civil War in the first half of the 1600s, the Puritans fought against the Crown and won, but were defeated again very quickly thereafter. Escape to the American colonies seemed the most prudent course of action.

The Puritans arrived on American shores in numbers far greater than the Pilgrims who preceded them. Their settlements were concentrated along the coast of New England, but extended as far south as Virginia. Their communities were governed by principles drawn directly from a literal reading of Scripture, believing that the Bible provided not only religious guidance but also a blueprint for civic governance.

In the Puritan colonies, citizenship was restricted to male church members. No one else was permitted a voice in government. Still, the political system was far more democratic than the monarchy that the colonists had left behind in England. Laws were derived from the Bible, with the Ten Commandments providing the principle template for right-living people. Punishments were based on scriptural example and were, in some cases, extremely harsh. Perhaps most important of all, these colonies harbored the hitherto unheard of conviction that civil society was also a moral society and that the moral precepts of the Bible were sufficient to create an enlightened community of men.

We are taught that this country was founded on the principle of "religious freedom," and to a very real extent this is true: The Pilgrims and Puritans came to America to escape religious persecution in their homeland. However, the modern assumption that "religious freedom" meant that all religions were treated equally is wrong. The early colonies were, without exception, Christian, and the principles on which they were based were drawn in large measure from the Bible. Thus, it is not an exaggeration to claim that America was, from its colonial beginnings, very much a Christian land.

To Form a New Nation

By the time a hundred years had passed, the small Christian settlements along America's Atlantic seaboard had grown to thirteen vibrant colonies with aspirations to independent nationhood. When the second Continental Congress of the American colonies was convened in the summer of 1776, the delegate Richard Henry Lee of Virginia at last publicly declared what many had been voicing privately—that the time for independence from England had arrived. The congressional delegates Thomas Jefferson, Benjamin Franklin, John Adams, and others formed a committee to draft a formal statement of this sentiment. The result was the Declaration of Independence, a key document in the history of America's journey toward nationhood.

The drafters of this document were not unanimous in their religious beliefs. Some professed no particular church affiliation, while others worshipped in one or another of the Protestant denominations that prevailed in the colonies. But all were inspired by an abiding spiritual commitment to Christian principles. The text of the declaration was expressly written "with a firm reliance on the Protection of Divine Providence." Although the language was kept rigorously nondenominational, nearly every line acknowledges the debt owed to divine creation, and the writers couch their assertions of essential rights to the operation of God's law. For the nation's founders, life, liberty, and the pursuit of happiness were God's gifts and not subject to revocation or restriction from some foreign sovereign.

When it came time to draft a constitution by which the newly formed United States of America would be governed, religious principles were once again very much in evidence. James Madison explicitly declared that the Ten Commandments were the foundation on which humankind must base its laws and system of government. Revolutionary heroes were equally explicit in declaring the source of their inspiration and faith. Patrick Henry, for instance, declared, "It cannot be emphasized too strongly or too often that this great nation was founded not by religionists but by Christians, not on religions but on the Gospel of Jesus Christ."

The Bill of Rights, another key document in the formation of the U.S. government, is often invoked to deny the Christian character of the nation. In particular, the first article of the bill, which asserts that "Congress shall make no law respecting an establishment of religion, or prohibiting the free exercise thereof," is commonly interpreted to mean that there can be no representation of religion—particularly Christianity—in the public sphere. In fact, that was not the intent of the founding fathers. Rather, this provision was drawn up in direct reference to the experience of the first colonists, who suffered persecution in England because they did not hew to state-ordered practices of worship. The controversies over whether or not a public school might display a Christmas nativity scene or a courthouse might hang the Ten Commandments on the wall were nowhere in the thoughts of the nation's founders. They wished only to prevent the establishment of a compulsory, federally mandated church.

Fidelity to our Christian heritage was reflected in all the early national documents, including the charters for each state's government. Even the designers of the nation's currency incorporated references to our debt to Christian scripture. Few legislative sessions, whether at the state or federal level, are convened before a Christian minister has offered a prayer for guidance, and even today our entire body of laws and the legal system itself are based on biblically derived principles.

Motto and Pledge

The signs and symbols of our sovereign nationhood were not created in a single moment, but developed over time. Nonetheless, the strong influence of our Christian founders remains a constant theme across the decades. Two examples are the creation of the national motto, "In God We Trust," which appears on our currency, and the national "Pledge of Allegiance."

The motto that appears on U.S. coins was first proposed during the nineteenth century, in the context of the American Civil War. The idea that American currency should include a reference to God was first proposed by the Reverend M. R. Watkinson, a Pennsylvania minister. During this era, when the upheavals of war and strife had brought grief and hardship to the whole nation, the American people were turning to their faith in God and Jesus with greater fervor than ever before, and Watkinson was merely expressing one way to encourage this spiritual reawakening. Watkinson's letter, received by the secretary of the treasury in 1861, did not offer any specific wording, however, so the director of the national mint was invited to draft a possible motto.

James Pollock was the director of the mint at that time. Pollock knew that the motto had to be brief, given the limited space available for inscription. He made two suggestions: "Our Country, Our God" and "Our God, Our Trust." He submitted his ideas to the Treasury Department for final review before sending it along to Congress for approval. Treasury Secretary Salmon P. Chase offered a minor change, from "Our God, Our Trust," to "In God We Trust." Congress accepted the design with Chase's change, and the motto first appeared on the 1864 issue of a two-cent coin.

The motto met with the approval of the public, and in the following years it was approved for inclusion on all coins minted in the United States. For the moment, however, it was merely an inscription on the nation's coinage. It did not rise to the status of the nation's official motto until nearly a century later. In July 1956, the Eighty-fourth Congress passed a resolution adopting the phrase as the national motto, and President Dwight D. Eisenhower signed it into law. In the following year, the motto was included as part of the design of the nation's paper currency as well as its coins.

Unlike the national motto, which arose from the express desire to acknowledge God's guidance, the "Pledge of Allegiance" began its existence with no reference to the Creator, even though it was written by a Baptist minister, Francis Bellamy. The original pledge, written in 1892 for use by public schools during their Columbus Day celebrations, was quite short: "I pledge allegiance to my flag and the Republic for which it stands, one nation, indivisible, with liberty and justice for all."

The pledge was adopted by the nation's public school system, and it became customary for students to recite it at the start of their day, before starting their lessons. In the 1920s, the wording was amended from "my flag" to "the flag of the United States of America," but the pledge then went another thirty years without further change.

In 1942, Congress enacted legislation that officially sanctioned the pledge as part of the U.S. Flag Code. In 1951, the Knights of Columbus mounted a campaign for one more change. This was a time of religious renewal, inspired in part by the fears of the cold war era, and some felt it would be appropriate to acknowledge the divine inspiration and protection on which the country was founded. Congress responded to this request by officially adding the words "under God" to the pledge. In 1954, President Eisenhower signed the legislation that made this final change a permanent part of the national pledge.

"O, Say, Can You See?"

Francis Scott Key, the composer of the song that became our national anthem, was a devout Christian and an active member of the Episcopal Church. In 1814, during the latter years of war with the British (known as the War of 1812) Key was practicing law in Washington, D.C. He learned that a colleague of his had been captured by the British, and he resolved to find a way to free his friend. With the help of President James Madison, a prisoner exchange was negotiated, and Key was one of the agents permitted to participate. During the course of the prisoner exchange, Key was detained temporarily on a British ship off the Maryland coast, from which vantage point he watched the British naval assault on Fort McHenry. The night battle, and the sight of the American flag flying valiantly above the fort, inspired him to write a poem that he titled "The Star Spangled Banner."

Most Americans know only the first verse of Key's inspirational anthem, but the original poem consists of four verses. The first verse celebrates the image of the flag and the valor of America's defenders, but it is in the final verse that Key gave full expression to his Christian convictions. That verse celebrates the United States as "this heaven-rescued land" and recognizes "the Power that has made and preserved us as a nation," concluding with the affirmation of the national motto, "In God is our trust."

Key's contribution to the civic life of our nation was not restricted to penning the national anthem. He was the driving force behind the American Sunday School Union, which fostered the establishment of religious instruction for children throughout the United States. He enlisted the support of several U.S. senators and congressmen, as well as the influential Daniel Webster, and enlisted missionaries to travel throughout the Mississippi River valley to establish Sunday schools in every town and city. By 1880, there were 61,299 schools offering instruction to more than 2.5 million children.

Patriotism and the Christian Hymn

The link between American patriotism and the Christian tradition is direct and based on the influence of our earliest colonial founders. The link is made explicit in the invocation of God in our founding documents and currency and in the wording of our national pledge and national anthem. But the connection between patriotism and Christianity is perhaps most movingly expressed in the form of our nation's patriotic hymns.

Samuel Francis Smith was born in Boston in 1808. Strongly called to the Baptist ministry, he attended Harvard and the Andover Theological Seminary, then went on to distinguish himself as a pastor, educator, writer, and editor of the *Baptist Missionary Magazine*. He was also a composer of hymns and composed more than 150 in the course of his lifetime. Smith was also a devoted patriot and in 1831, while still only a student, he was moved to combine his patriotic fervor with his profound faith to compose a hymn. Borrowing the tune of the British national anthem ("God Save the Queen"), he sat down and wrote the opening words, "My country 'tis of thee, sweet land of liberty, of thee I sing." The hymn, simply titled "America," directly invokes our Christian heritage ("Pilgrim's pride") and the closing verse opens with a direct homage to the Creator, "Our father's God, to Thee, Author of liberty, to Thee we sing."

Julia Ward Howe was an abolitionist, a suffragist, and a member of the Transcendentalist movement of the time. A Unitarian, she was somewhat iconoclastic in her beliefs, but was nonetheless profoundly moved by the example of Christ as humankind's savior. While visiting a Union army encampment during the American Civil War, she noted that the soldiers amused themselves by singing the somewhat bawdy tune "John Brown's Body." She disapproved of the lyrics, but felt the tune to which they were sung was extremely inspirational, and in 1861 she set her hand to composing more uplifting lyrics. The result was one of our nation's best-known and beloved patriotic hymns, "The Battle Hymn of the Republic."

In 1904, another patriotic hymn was added to our cultural heritage, authored by the daughter of a Congregationalist minister in Falmouth, Massachusetts. Katharine Lee Bates was born in 1859, studied at Wellesley College, and pursued a career as a poet and educator. In 1895, she published the poem "America the Beautiful" in her father's church newsletter. Not content with the verses, she revised them over the next ten years and submitted the final version for publication in the *Boston Transcript* in 1904. The poem, which so movingly combined patriotic sentiment with a profound religious sensibility, quickly gained widespread public acceptance. A number of attempts to match the words to music were tried over the next two decades. The most familiar version employs the tune "Materna," composed by Samuel A. Ward. Its simple lyrics and direct acknowledgment of God's grace have inspired many efforts to make this our national anthem (an honor bestowed on Francis Scott Key's "Star Spangled Banner" by President Herbert Hoover in 1931).

V

FOUNDERS OF THE FAITH

Throughout the centuries, Christianity has undergone many changes, as humankind has struggled to fully understand and implement the teachings of our Lord. While every Christian makes an important contribution to the faith, a few individuals stand out in the history of the church as having played key roles in the development of the greater Christian tradition.

First and foremost of these, of course, were Jesus's early disciples. Without them, the church would not have survived the years of persecution under the Roman emperors during the first 300 years of its existence. Second would be the Roman emperor Constantine, whose conversion to Christianity in A.D. 313 permitted the church to come out of hiding and spread throughout the world. But over time the church became caught up in the politics of the world, and the religious movement that Jesus founded on the faith of the common people became the province of the elite. It wasn't until the sixteenth century that a new movement arose that sought to reclaim the faith for the people to whom Jesus originally ministered. This was the Reformation, and the men who led that movement, as well as those who built on its successes, contributed much to what we understand as the Christian tradition today.

Martin Luther

Martin Luther was born in Eiselben, Germany, on November 10, 1483. His father began as a farmer, but set out to improve the family fortunes by embarking on a career in copper mining. Luther grew up in a prosperous Catholic household and, as befitted his social station, was educated in the church. Early on, he felt the call to the religious life and at first was determined to become a monk in the teaching order of the Augustinians. He was duly ordained and took on the duties of an educator at the University of Wittenberg as well as serving as a priest and confessor in the Wittenberg parish.

Luther was a man of great spiritual curiosity and profound faith, and he soon became disturbed by what he believed to be abuses of the faith by the Catholic Church in which he served. Most upsetting to him was the church practice of selling indulgences. This practice permitted a parishioner to essentially buy his or her way out of sin by making a hefty payment to the priests. This practice enraged Luther, who believed it was an abominable corruption of Christ's message and mission. Not one to stand by quietly in the face of injustice, Luther wrote a letter to his superiors, taking them to task for the sale of indulgences and other abuses he saw in the practices of the Catholic Church. When he received no response to his letter, he nailed it, known as the "95 Theses," to the doors of the Castle Church in Wittenberg.

Church officials ignored Luther's rebellion at first, but when he refused to let the matter drop, a number of his superiors finally decided that something needed to be done. In 1521, his protests against indulgences and other churchly abuses became intolerable, and he was declared a heretic and banished from the church. He went into hiding to avoid arrest by the agents of the Inquisition and began his work on translating the New Testament from Latin into the German language, so that the holy scripture would no longer be the monopoly of the priesthood.

In exile, Luther remained active in the practice of his understanding of Christian faith. He composed many hymns and spent much time and thought on the subject of the true faith and the proper means by which it should be practiced. He wrote extensively on the subject, and his writings inspired other reform-minded Christians throughout Europe to break away from the Catholic Church. When English reformers sought to emulate his translation of the Bible into the common tongue, he was often called on for advice and counsel. Thus, it can be said that he not only inspired the creation of the Lutheran denomination of Protestantism but also that he was instrumental in the birth of all the other forms of Protestant worship that arose during this era.

John Calvin

John Calvin was born in the town of Noyen, France, on July 10, 1509, into a comfortably successful family. He was well educated and trained for a career in the legal profession, like his father before him, but he also took courses in theology and in the biblical languages of Greek and Hebrew. Through the influence of his father, who was familiar with the writings of Martin Luther, Calvin began to explore the ideas championed by the Reformation movement. Soon, he began to write on the subject, suggesting reforms of his own, and in so doing he angered the elders of the powerful French Catholic establishment.

Calvin was forced to flee the country to avoid arrest and possible execution for heresy. He traveled around Europe, settling for a time in Basel, Switzerland. There, he began to write his major theological work, *Institution de la religion Chrétienne*. This master work would take him thirty years to complete.

From Basel, Calvin moved to the Swiss capital of Geneva, where he became active in the local Protestant movement. Unlike elsewhere in

Europe, the Geneva Protestants were successful in eventually taking political control. Calvin remained there and opened his home as a refuge to religious reformists from England, France, and Germany who sought protection from prosecution in their home countries. In the late 1530s, however, Calvin became involved in a political movement that aimed to install a theocracy in Geneva. The movement failed, and Calvin was forced, once again, into exile. He went to Germany for a time, but was finally allowed to return to Geneva in 1541.

Calvin's beliefs, outlined in his master theological work, placed primary emphasis on the literal scriptures. He also believed strongly in the concept of predestination and rejected the authority of the papacy. In addition, he held that by faith alone was it possible to achieve salvation, even in the absence of good works. He was an advocate of simplicity in worship and did not approve of the incorporation of music during church services, preferring instead poetry in the form of Psalms. His ideas on the proper organization of the church did away with much of the traditional Catholic hierarchy and placed authority in the hands of trusted members of each congregation.

Calvin's theology provided the foundation for the Protestant denomination that bears his name. In France, his teachings were spread by the Huguenots, who eventually were forced to leave the country and establish settlements in North America. His theology also informed the doctrine of both the Puritan and Pilgrim movements, as well as the Baptist Church, and traces of his theology were reflected in a great many other Protestant groups of his time as well.

John Knox

John Knox was born into a Scottish Catholic family in the early 1500s (sources differ as to the year of his birth, with both 1505 and 1513 being mentioned). His training was for the priesthood, but early in his career he became seriously troubled by the corruption he saw in the church. He came across the teachings of Martin Luther and was drawn to the sentiments he found therein. He began advocating for reform, but at that time the Scottish rulers were strongly allied to the French royal house, which was rigidly Catholic. He was soon arrested for his views and forced into the equivalent of slave labor.

His story might have ended there, but for the fact that a reform-minded king, Edward VI, occupied the English throne. King Edward negotiated for Knox's release and offered the renegade priest sanctuary in England. Unfortunately, Edward was succeeded on the throne by Mary Tudor, who was rabidly anti-Protestant. Knox was forced to flee to Europe to avoid being arrested again.

During this time of exile, Knox eventually found his way to Geneva, where John Calvin was known to offer sanctuary to members of the reformation movement. Knox stayed at Calvin's home for a time, where he had the chance to learn firsthand the church reforms advocated by his host. Knox found Calvin's theological doctrine and practices very persuasive, and when he was finally able to return to Scotland in 1559 he set about putting them into practice.

Although Knox strove to remain true to Calvin's teachings, he did contribute an original embellishment. He took Calvin's concept of church governance by a council of elders (a form of representative democracy) and formed the Scottish Reformed Church. At the local level, the councils were called presbyteries, at the regional level they were called synods, and at the national level they were known as general assemblies. This organizational innovation eventually gave rise to the name by which we know Knox's church: Presbyterianism.

Knox died in 1572, but not before he saw his church expand to the American colonies. The settlements, concentrated around the areas now known as New York, New Jersey, and Pennsylvania, quickly grew in wealth and influence. Many credit the Presbyterians of later years with contributing the concept of representational democracy to the Constitutional Congresses that gave rise to the new American nation.

John and Charles Wesley

John Wesley was born in Epworth, England, on June 17, 1703, one of fifteen children born to Anglican clergyman Samuel Wesley. He was raised with the expectation that he would follow his father into the clergy and was admitted to the priesthood of the Church of England in 1728. He joined the faculty of Oxford University in 1729, where he became a member of the Holy Club, an organization devoted to the spiritual development of its members through the performance of charitable works with society's less fortunate. During this period, he made the acquaintance of George Whitefield, with whom he had many long talks on the subject of theology.

Dissatisfied with the life of an academic, Wesley elected to become a missionary. He was posted to the Americas, with the assignment of establishing a mission in the territory now known as the state of Georgia. En route to his assignment he had his first encounter with representatives of the German evangelical movement known as the Moravians and was intrigued by their approach to Christian worship. When he was recalled to England 1738 at the end of his missionary assignment, he made a point of seeking out the small Moravian congregation that had been established in London to learn more about its doctrine.

At about this time, Wesley renewed his acquaintance with Whitefield, who was visiting London. Whitefield had spent the previous years as an evangelist, preaching the Gospels throughout the English countryside. Whitefield had broken with the Anglican church and was now advocating a form of Calvinism. He persuaded Wesley to join him on his next evangelical foray into rural England and introduced his Anglican friend to the rewards of sermonizing in the open air to appreciative crowds.

As a result of Wesley's exploration of Moravian and Calvinist doctrine, he eventually was moved to break with the Anglican church. In 1739 he recruited a few like-minded colleagues and founded the first Methodist society. Although his church movement was largely independent, it at first maintained close ties with both Whitefield's Calvinist organization and the Moravian society. However, Wesley could never reconcile himself with the idea of predestination, which was central to Calvinism, and he had similar disagreements with several points of Moravian doctrine, so in 1740 he cut all ties with both groups. His movement found many followers both in England and in the United States. A profound believer in education, he wrote prolifically and made certain that his works were priced low enough to be affordable by the widest possible audience.

Charles Wesley was younger than his brother, John, by five years. He followed the same educational and career path and was an early supporter of John's emerging Methodist movement, following an intensely felt spiritual awakening in 1738. He did not share his brother's taste for public life, however, and was uncomfortable as a preacher, even though his sermons were enthusiastically received. Charles made his own original contribution to Methodism, however, through his gifts as a composer of hymns, carols, and religious poems. He wrote more than 5,500 of them, including the beloved Christmas standard "Hark, the Herald Angels Sing." He died in 1788. His brother, John, died three years later.

VI

FAMILY MATTERS

At the heart of the American Christian experience is the family. It is within the family that each of us lives out the teachings of Jesus on a day-to-day basis, and it is here that we pass our faith down along the generations. The primacy of relationships between husband and wife and parents and children is recognized throughout the Old Testament and is explicitly celebrated in the teachings of Jesus and the later writings of the apostles. Christians today also recognize the essential nature of strong family values informed by faith.

The central importance of the concept of family to the Christian tradition is based on the understanding that the household represents a microcosmic instance of the fundamental relationship between Christians and God, as mediated through Jesus.

Little wonder, then, that the Old Testament writers used the relationship between God and His faithful as a model for the relationships that should exist within the human household. Jesus, in His teachings, often turned that analogy around, using the familiar relationships of the household to illustrate the proper relationship that should exist between His own followers and God. In our daily lives, we can enhance our own spiritual growth by putting the teachings of the Gospel into practice in our family relationships.

Christianity and Childhood

In scripture, there is perhaps no one stage of human life more consistently valued than childhood. During Christ's ministry, He frequently used the example of children, and the qualities we associate with childhood, as a guide for how even adults should approach worship. We find this clearly expressed in Matthew 18:1, when Jesus says, "unless you are converted and become like children, you will never enter the kingdom of Heaven."

According to the Bible, children are the gift of God, and families without children are bereft. Still, for all its celebration of children, the Bible also sets high standards for their deportment.

In the Christian household, there is an established order of responsibilities that is ordained by Scripture. Children are to be cherished and nurtured, but they also owe obedience to the authority of the parent. In Ephesians 6:1, Paul writes, "Children, obey your parents in the Lord, for this is right." The modern trend in secular households to indulge children (called child-centered families) is one that would surely fill Paul with dismay. Paul's message of obedience is echoed in 1 Peter 5:5, when the younger members of a clan are told to "submit yourselves unto the elder." Obedience and submission are important, because they reflect the important virtue of humility, and it is within the relationships of the family that this, like all other virtues, are best learned.

But this is not to say that children are mere slaves to the quixotic whims of their parents. Scripture admonishes parents that they must combine authority with mercy and understanding, just as God the Father does for us, His human creation.

Within Christianity, children do have obligations, foremost among which is found in the fifth commandment, "Honor thy father and mother." Within the Christian tradition, it is the paramount duty of children to show respect to the parents who nuture them. And they must learn—in particular, they must be open to learning about their faith. This last injunction is not solely directed at children, however—it creates a significant responsibility for the parents as well.

Still, children are held in a special place in Jesus's heart. In Matthew 18:4–5, Jesus shows how His special love for the vulnerable and the helpless is reflected in His attitudes toward children, "Therefore, whoever humbles himself like this child, that one is the greatest in the kingdom of Heaven. And whoever welcomes one child like this in My name, welcomes Me."

The Homeschooling Movement

Christian homeschooling has been in existence throughout this nation's history. For much of this time, homeschooling was a necessity, not a choice, particularly in rural or frontier areas that lacked teachers or school facilities. Most early schooling, whether conducted at home or in a community school, was Bible based, for this was often the only book that households could afford. With the rise of the public school system, however, homeschooling was discouraged and, in places, even outlawed.

In the 1960s, however, the educator John Holt wrote a number of books chronicling the decline in the quality of teaching in the public schools. His widely read analyses encouraged a number of groups to undertake the homeschooling of their children, especially conservative Christian groups that were already disaffected by the secular nature of public education. By the end of the 1960s, homeschooling was a rapidly growing phenomenon.

For Christian households, homeschooling offered a number of

advantages. First, it allowed them greater control over their children's exposure to objectionable elements of the broader national culture. Second, it permitted them more oversight over the instructional materials—texts, videos, and so forth—that would be used. For Christian homeschoolers of the period, the most important advantage was that they could build all lessons around the Bible, a teaching strategy that was not allowed in the state-run public schools.

As the public school system continued to decline during the next two decades, conservative Christian homeschoolers were joined by many other families. Crumbling schools, an escalation of in-school violence, and squabbles among educational experts over teaching philosophies drove many new families into the homeschool movement. By their sheer increase in numbers, homeschoolers finally had some political power, and before the end of the 1980s they had succeeded in getting independent homeschooling legalized in forty states. The remaining ten states permitted schooling at home, but required a state-certified teacher to oversee lesson plans and conduct periodic progress tests. By the mid-1990s, independent homeschooling was legal in all fifty states.

Over these decades of development, a number of organizations were created to provide support and assistance to homeschooling families. Publications such as *Home Education Magazine* and *Teaching Home Magazine* provided homeschoolers with news of the latest developments in the movement and access to teaching materials, and gave homeschooling parents a venue in which to communicate with one another. With the proliferation of home computers and the rise of the Internet, homeschoolers could avail themselves of a wide range of advice and resources with increasing ease.

In the 1990s, however, Christian homeschoolers began to advocate for faith-based separation within the movement. Their publications and service providers sought to keep a specifically Christian orientation for all texts and lesson plans. In particular, the Christian homeschoolers found too much secular humanist influence creeping into educational materials and rejected the then increasingly popular child-centered childrearing philosophy that advocated catering to children's wishes.

In response, a companion movement to Christian homeschooling began to gain momentum. This was the home-centered living movement, of which Mary Pride was (and remains) a leading voice. Basing their philosophies on a strict reading of the Bible, proponents of this movement advocated removal of homeschooled children from contact with all non-Christian influences. In compliance with this movement, *Teaching Home Magazine* began to require all of its article writers, as well as all resource suppliers who wished to advertise in its pages, to sign a statement of faith committing themselves to following a set of established, Bible-centered guidelines in all their work or products.

Non-Christian and more liberal Christian homeschoolers were not left without resources, however. Inclusive support groups, such as the National Homeschool Association, continued to provide for their needs. However, the conservative Christian homeschoolers have grown to become the largest and most powerful faction in the overall movement. Some fear that the divisiveness and contentiousness within the larger movement may constitute a threat to the independence currently enjoyed by homeschoolers. They warn of increasing pressure on public officials to enact and enforce regulations on the movement.

Motherhood

We all know that lovely Mother's Day poem that begins "M is for the million things she gave me." Written by Howard Johnson and set to music by Theodore Morse in 1915, it reflects the Christian belief that motherhood is an essential role, deserving of the highest respect. The mother's importance is equal to that of the father, as can be seen in Exodus 20:12, where we find the fifth commandment specifying, "Honor thy father and mother." For all Christians, the highest example of the self-sacrifice, devotion, support, and care that are encompassed in a mother's love is to be found in Mary, the mother of Jesus.

Throughout scripture, we learn of the honor due to good mothers, and we learn why. In Proverbs 31, we read that "Her children arise up, and call her blessed; her husband also, and he praiseth her." Scripture informs us that a mother's love is all-forgiving, born from the years of nurturing her children and lasting throughout their lives. Isaiah 49:15 says, "Can a woman forget her sucking child, that she should not have compassion on the son of her womb?"

The story of Sarah, the wife of Abraham, illustrates the great joy but also the responsibility of motherhood, for she was promised to be "a mother of nations; kings of people shall be of her" (Genesis 17:17). The Christian mother understands that, like Sarah, the children she nurtures are filled with promise and that she bears much of the responsibility to see that they someday fulfill that promise. She must be protector and peacekeeper, as Rebekah tried to be when she interceded between her sons, Esau and Jacob (Genesis 27:44–45).

Mary, the mother of Jesus, provides our most familiar example of motherhood—both its joys and sacrifice. Throughout Jesus's life she was at His side, and she suffered the mother's ultimate sacrifice when He gave His life to save us all. As He honored His mother, so also must we honor ours, every day of the year. One Methodist minister's daughter, however, was determined to gain official recognition for all mothers, everywhere.

Anna M. Jarvis was born in 1864 in Webster, West Virginia. Her mother, Ann Marie, not only raised a large family (there were eleven children in all), but as a minister's wife she also found time to support his church work. She taught Bible study and founded the first Mothers Day Work Club, an organization that spread throughout the region in the years before the Civil War. One day, as she was teaching a class on "Mothers of the Bible," Ann Marie expressed the wish that society some day would formally recognize the service and sacrifice that mothers make every day of their lives. Anna was only twelve years old at the time, but she never forgot her own mother's wish.

Anna followed her mother's example by becoming a teacher. She never married, but lived at her mother's side until Ann Marie's death in 1905. From that day onward, Anna Jarvis dedicated herself to fulfilling her mother's wish. She enlisted the Mothers Day Work Clubs and launched a letter-writing campaign to local and national legislators. At last, however, she found a powerful ally to her cause: the wealthy Philadelphia philanthropist John Wanamaker. By 1909, forty-five states officially recognized May 10 as Mothers Day, and by 1914 President Woodrow Wilson approved a congressional resolution setting aside the second Sunday each May for a national day of celebration of motherhood.

Fatherhood

In the Christian tradition, the father stands at the head of the family, in the position of patriarch. It might be said that he occupies a position within the household that is analogous to the role of God over His creation. But this comparison must not be taken too far. In scripture, the concepts of humility and obedience on the part of wife and children are tempered by the responsibility of the father to exercise his authority wisely and with justice. As the traditional disciplinarian, it is incumbent on the father to administer justice firmly but even-handedly.

In the modern Christian family, which faces the same economic pressures as everyone else, it is sometimes difficult to cling to traditional roles. Mothers are at times forced to augment the family income by working outside the home, but the idea of father as breadwinner remains the ideal. Whenever it is possible to live this ideal, traditional Christian families do tend to favor it, but if they are true to scriptural teachings, the father's duties do not stop at bringing in the paycheck. He is also expected to offer emotional support and a positive example for his children.

As is true in all corners of modern society, Christian fatherhood is facing something of a crisis. Divorce rates in the Christian community are as high as among non-Christians, which means that many children are being raised with little or no access to their father's presence and example. Christian organizations have responded to this challenge, out of concern that the lack of a father's participation in the household may lead to significant personal and spiritual problems for children later on. Within individual churches, men's ministries have been formed to strengthen the father-child bonds that can be weakened by divorce or at the very least to provide alternative masculine authority figures to whom such children can turn.

Marriage

Marriage is the cornerstone institution of Christian society. Its importance derives in large part because it was ordained by God Himself, when He bound Adam to Eve before their fall from grace. The verses attesting to this first marriage are Genesis 2:18–24, and within these verses several significant aspects of what constitutes a proper marriage are identified for the first time.

First is the aspect of companionship, "God said, it is not good that man should be alone; I will create a helpmeet for him." This is the reason behind God's decision to create Eve from Adam's rib, because He knew that man, His creation, was a social being who needed a partner with whom to go through life. There is no disputing that this first human pair was married because Adam recites the words that, in the New Testament, serve as the final charge in a formal marriage ceremony, "Therefore shall a man leave his father and his mother and cleave unto his wife, and they shall be one flesh (Genesis 2:24)."

That last verse also speaks to the second essential aspect of Christian marriage: It is intended to be a lifetime commitment. Whatever doubts one might have on this score are cleared away in the New Testament, when in Matthew 4–6 Jesus responds to a question about divorce by repeating Adam's own pledge and adding, "What therefore God has joined together, let not man put asunder." The bond between man and woman is for life.

A further reason for the institution of marriage is to prevent immorality. For Adam and Eve, before they were expelled from the Garden of Eden, this was perhaps not a paramount practical concern, but it was of profound spiritual import. Once made, a vow cannot be unmade without a breach of faith. Honor is an attribute of great value in the Christian ethic. Out in the world of men, the practical consequences of immorality—whether through promiscuity or adultery—were and still are too grave to justify self-indulgence. We see it in the modern world, with divorce rates soaring and single parents desperately trying to do the job of two. Only through the institution of marriage can a stable family be formed in which children may best be nurtured.

The apostle Paul had much to offer in clarifying the marital relationship. It is, fundamentally, a partnership. In Ephesians 5:33, Paul says, "Each of you [men] must love his wife as he loves himself, and the wife must respect the husband." In 1 Corinthians 7:4, he goes on to add, "The wife's body does not belong to her alone but also to her husband. In the same way, the husband's body does not belong to him alone, but also to his wife." The implication is that they share a reciprocal relationship, albeit one in which each is assigned different roles.

Paul frequently uses the term *submission* when speaking about the role of wives. This is a concept that many women today find difficult to accept. But it is important to realize that Paul does not stop at enjoining wives to submit to their husbands. In Ephesians 5:21, he makes it clear that submission is required of both spouses, "Submit to one another out of reverence for Christ."

Throughout the Old and New Testaments, passages dealing with marriage and the responsibilities of husbands and wives keep coming back to the mutuality of the relationship. Husbands and wives are admonished repeatedly that they should treat one another with tenderness and respect, to refrain from harsh treatment of one another, and to show patience, even in difficult times.

If we accept the union of Adam and Eve as God's model for human relationships, it is clear that monogamy was the original intent. Even so, there were periods chronicled in the Old Testament when men were permitted more than one wife. For Christians, the teachings of Jesus and the apostles make it clear that, regardless of the polygamous practices of some Old Testament figures, the law of monogamy was restored with the coming of Christ. It is reaffirmed in Matthew 19:5 and 1 Corinthians 6:16.

In recent years, there has been much controversy in the media over the extension of the right to marriage to gay and lesbian couples. From a biblical perspective, this is not an option. If we take it as a given that the model for marriage was provided by Adam and Eve, then marriage must involve a man and a woman. In addition, the Bible does not acknowledge homosexuality as legitimate, and in the Old Testament it even advocates harsh punishment for the practice (see Leviticus). While it may be argued that Jesus, in His teachings, sometimes offered a gentler alternative to many things that were ordained in earlier times, there is no evidence that He ever relaxed the prohibitions against homosexuality.

VII

A FIELD TRIP TO THE HOLY LAND

For many Christians, there is nothing more moving than to walk the same streets and byways that Jesus trod two millennia ago. The places He knew in life, and those of key significance to the early Christians who struggled to build His church, may lie in far-off lands, but they call out to us, nonetheless. Not everyone can experience the special joy of visiting these holy places in person, but we can all enrich our understanding of His life and mission by learning more about the world in which He lived.

Bethlehem

Everyone knows that Bethlehem was the birthplace of Jesus, but its biblical significance far predates the coming of Christianity. The town was home to a small clan in the kingdom of Judah, far enough away from the centers of power that it might have remained an unknown backwater, forgotten by history. But even in the earliest books of the Old Testament, Bethlehem is singled out for mention, even if only in passing, and in the book of Micah (5:2), written sometime between 735 and 700 B.C., come the first intimations of the great role this little town will someday play, "Bethlehem Ephrathat, you are small among the clans of Judah. One will come from you to rule over Israel for Me. His origin is from antiquity, eternity."

Dusty little Bethlehem, which lay just six miles from the city of Jerusalem, was just a place that people passed through on their way to somewhere else for the earliest years of its existence. But long before the prophecy of Micah, a clan of kinsmen arose to pave the way for the coming of Jesus. Boaz of Bethlehem took to wife a woman named Ruth sometime around 1100 B.C. Together, they had children, including a son named Jesse. Jesse, in turn, was father to David. David was born in Bethlehem and lived there as a simple shepherd until he was taken into the household of Judah's current king, Saul. He retained fond memories of the town of his birth even after he left it and even after he succeeded Saul as king. Along with Jerusalem, Bethlehem has come to be known as the "city of David."

David's royal lineage continued on through the generations, and among the great king's many descendants was a man named Joseph, who was also born in Bethlehem but who, as a grown man, lived in Nazareth and worked as a carpenter. In those times, the kingdom of Judah was a subject state within the Roman Empire, and taxes were assessed each year to raise the tribute payments that Rome demanded. The tribute was assessed according to the number of citizens of each of Rome's subject states, which meant that a census had to be held every so often to determine the amount of tribute that must be paid and the amount of taxes each citizen owed. During the census, every adult male had to register in the town of his birth, so, in the year that Joseph and his young wife were anxiously awaiting the birth of their first child, they had to return to Bethlehem.

We all know the rest of the story, immortalized in our Christmas traditions. With no room in any of the town's inns, the young couple was forced to shelter for the night in a stable—actually a cave in which domestic animals were kept. During the reign of the Roman emperor Constantine, after his conversion to Christianity, he ordered the construction of a massive church near the cave in which Jesus was born. It stood for more than 200 years, but was then destroyed by a fire. Over its ruins, and preserving some of the original tile flooring, a new church was erected by the emperor Justinian during the sixth century. Justinian's church still stands, surviving even the wanton destruction of the Persians when they attacked the empire in the seventh century and ruthlessly attacked Christian churches wherever they found them. The cave itself also remains largely intact and is the destination of many faithful Christians every Christmas season.

The town of Bethlehem was not so lucky. It was largely destroyed during the violence of the Christian Crusades against the Muslims who held the Holy Land during the first century of the first millenium. The crusaders rebuilt it, but it was destroyed again in the next century when the Turks attempted to reclaim the town. Over the centuries, Christians, Jews, and Muslims have all laid claim to the town, for it figures importantly in all three traditions. Today, it is a part of the state of Israel, but its population reflects all three ethnic and religious traditions.

Catacombs of Rome

In Rome at the time of Christ and in the years immediately following, the custom was to cremate the dead. Christians, however, preferred to entomb their dead, as Jesus Himself was buried, and saw cremation as a pagan practice. For the wealthy followers of Jesus, it was customary to bury the dead on family land, but Christ's mission was one that embraced the poor, who had no land. Sometime between 100 and 150 Christians began burying their dead in underground chambers linked by galleries, which we know today by the Greek word *catacombs*.

The catacombs consist of long tunnels laid out in a maze, and along the walls niches were cut out to receive the shrouded bodies of the dead. Once the body was laid to rest in its niche, the opening was covered with marble or tiles, and the burial niche was marked with the name of the deceased and, in most cases, with a symbol of Christ: The sign of the fish, the sign of the anchor, and the sign of the peacock all appear on the catacomb walls. The earliest catacombs grew from the established burial sites of landed Christian families. Over time, Christians collected money to buy additional land for the creation of more such burial sites. Today, we know of more than sixty catacombs in the lands around Rome (burials were forbidden within the imperial city). Some of the tunnel networks extend a hundred miles or more and, all told, they provide a final resting place for tens of thousands of Christians.

The catacombs certainly saw many burial rituals, and at times during the early centuries they provided a place where Christians could gather to celebrate communion without fear of persecution. During the era of persecution, they offered one of the few places where Christian art could be made and displayed. When the emperor Constantine converted to Christianity and the faithful were free to profess their religion openly, some of the burial sites that housed martyrs became true shrines, and pilgrims from throughout the expanding territory of Christendom came to pay their respects.

With the start of the fifth century, Christians ended the practice of burial in the catacombs and established cemeteries above ground. Still, the catacombs continued to draw crowds of pilgrims interested in honoring the tombs of fallen martyrs. Toward the end of the eighth century, however, the church feared for the safety of these important relics, because Rome faced repeated barbarian attacks. The remains of the early martyrs were removed from the catacombs and reburied in various churches around the city. Pilgrims ceased to come, and the catacombs fell into disrepair. Over time, they were forgotten.

They were rediscovered in the middle of the sixteenth century by the Italian scholar Antonio Bosio. Over the next four centuries, archaeologists have excavated significant portions of several catacombs, and five have been opened to the public. These are known by the names of the martyrs who were once interred within their walls: Saint Agnes, Priscilla, Domitilla, Saint Sebastian, and Saint Calliatus. The archaeological excavation of the catacombs is under the supervision and control of the Pope, through the offices of the Pontifical Commission of Sacred Archaeology.

Jerusalem

Jerusalem was a thriving urban center long before it fell under the rule of the kingdom of Judah. Before 1010 B.C., it was held by a people called the Jebusites, against whom King David was waging war. When he conquered the city, he decided to make it the capital of his kingdom. During his reign, he brought the Ark of the Covenant here and enclosed the city within defensive walls. David's reign from Jerusalem was continued by his successor, Solomon, who built his temple there. It remained the capital of the kingdom of Judah until 586, when it was seized by the army of Babylon, which destroyed the Temple of Solomon when it captured the city.

The Babylonians could not hold on to their prize for long. They were conquered, in turn, by the Persian armies of Cyrus the Great, who found it politically expedient to show favor to the Jews. He restored to them their capital, but not their independence. They were now a tributory state of the Persian Empire and served as governors rather than as kings. During this period, the Temple of Solomon was rebuilt by Governor

Zerubbabel in 515 B.C. The Old Testament book of Ezra offers insights into this period of the city's history.

By the second century B.C., Jerusalem was subject to the rule of Syria, which was ruled by Antiochus IV. The Syrian king persecuted the city's Jews and desecrated the temple. A priest named Mattathias led a revolt against this treatment, and his son, Judas Maccabeus, carried on the battle after Mattathias's death in 166 B.C. Judas reclaimed Jerusalem and restored the Temple of Solomon to its former glory. Years of fighting with Syria followed, taking the life of Judas and his two brothers, Jonathan and Simon. One of Simon's sons finally succeeded in bringing the conflict to an end, but after his death the region once again slipped into war. Finally, in 63 B.C. Rome sent Pompey to intervene, and he annexed the entire territory in the name of the Roman Empire. The Romans appointed their own governors, and they were not inclined to favor the independent-minded descendants of Judas Maccabeus. Instead, Pompey elevated the family of Herod to the governorship of Judea. It was during the reign of the Herods that Jesus was born and, later, brought His message to the city of Jerusalem.

Jesus first came to Jerusalem at the age of twelve, when His parents brought Him to the temple for His coming-of-age ritual, the bar mitzvah. During this visit, Jesus was recognized for the first time as the Messiah by a devout man named Simeon and a prophetess named Anna. During this visit, the young Jesus slipped away from His parents and was found later lecturing the elders of the temple. When Mary, His mother, questioned Him, He announced His mission on earth for the first time.

Jesus returned to Jerusalem several times after He began His ministry in earnest. His last visit precipitated the events that led to His crucifixion. He died there, was entombed just outside the city, and it is in Jerusalem that He appeared to His disciples after His death. For all these reasons, Jerusalem stands at the heart of the Christian tradition and is, with Bethlehem, one of the two most important places on earth to all who profess the faith. Thus, when Jerusalem fell to Islam in the eleventh century, all Christendom was appalled. The European nations, all led by Christian rulers, declared the First Crusade to reclaim the city, and finally succeeded in taking it in 1099. For the next 170 years, control of the city slipped back and forth between Christians and Muslims. In 1291, the Eighth Crusade (the last one) ended in victory for Islam. From then on, until 1917, it remained outside of Christian control.

Jerusalem, along with the rest of Palestine, was occupied by British forces in 1917, during World War I. It was made the administrative capital of the region, which was set to be partitioned among its various peoples: Jews, Christians, and (in the majority) Muslims and Arabs. Recognizing the importance of the city of Jerusalem to all three religious traditions, the United Nations sought to internationalize it, so that it would not fall under the authority of any one group. The majority bloc of Arabs and Muslims rejected the plan in 1949. In 1967, Israel resolved the issue by capturing the city, along with other territories, during the Six-Day War. The fate of Jerusalem remains contested today.

Nazareth

Bethlehem was a relatively small town in the kingdom of Judah, but compared to Nazareth it was a bustling metropolis. More a village than a town, Nazareth lay about fifteen miles from the shores of the Sea of Galilee, and its inhabitants were, by and large, farmers. Far from any trade routes, the dozen or so families who lived there had little contact with the outside world. On the face of such evidence, there is no reason at all why we should ever have heard of such an insignificant little place.

But Nazareth was the home of a young woman named Mary, who was engaged to a man from Bethlehem named Joseph. No one knows what might have inspired Joseph to move to this backwater town, but it was here that he plied his trade as a carpenter and that he met the woman he was determined to make his wife. Six months into their engagement, young Mary received a visitation from the Holy Spirit and learned the momentous news that she was with child and that she should name him Jesus.

Before their child was born, Joseph and Mary were forced by the laws of tax and census to leave Nazareth and return to the city of Joseph's birth. The town lapsed back into its accustomed obscurity and might have stayed that way. But Herod the Great, the governor of Judea, had heard rumors that a child was to be born in Bethlehem that would one day become "King of the Jews"—the title that he lay claim to for himself. He ordered the massacre of all boys under one year of age, forcing Joseph and Mary to flee with their newborn son into Egypt. When Herod died, the young family felt it might be safe enough to return to their homeland, but they did not dare to go to Bethlehem. Instead, they went to the town where Mary was born, a town so far from the bustle of the outside world that they could be sure that no one would look for them there. That town was Nazareth.

Jesus spent His childhood in this small, sleepy town. It was here that, as a youth, He heard rumors of a great prophet who was traveling throughout Judea prophesying and baptizing. It was from here that He set forth, on the verge of His ministry, to spend forty days and forty nights in the wilderness, fasting and searching for inspiration and overcoming the temptations that Satan set in His way. It was to Nazareth that Jesus began His ministry, but His message fell on deaf ears, and so He moved on, beginning His long journey throughout Judea to share His gospel of faith and hope.

Because of all these associations, the town of Nazareth was important to Christians from the earliest days of the church. Once Christianity was recognized by Rome and began to spread throughout the empire, it became a destination for pilgrims, who came from all parts of the imperial world. Like Jerusalem, Nazareth fell to Muslim rule in the eleventh century and was one of the prizes over which crusaders and Muslims fought from 1099 to 1291, when the forces of Islam succeeded in ejecting the European crusaders from the region. It slumbered under first Syrian, then Turkish rule, but under the Ottoman Empire permission was granted for the Franciscan order of the Christian church to take charge of the town and build a church. In 1917, when the British claimed the lands of Palestine, Nazareth knew a period of respite, and in 1948 it became a part of the newly created state of Israel. It remains a predominantly agricultural town, but it has grown much in the last decades. Where tradition holds that Mary was born, a church now commemorates the site. Pilgrims of every Christian denomination visit each year, much as their predecessors did during the days of the early church.

Neot Kedumim

Midway between Tel Aviv and Jerusalem, in the state of Israel, is a place called Neot Kedumim, the labor of love created by Dr. Ephraim and Hannah Hareuveni, who were emigrés from Russia in the 1920s. They established the Museum of Biblical and Talmudic Botany in Israel. What they dreamed of, however, was to someday create a botanical preserve in which they would grow all the plants mentioned in the Old and New Testaments. They did not live to see their dreams realized, but in 1965, their son, Nogah, applied to the Israeli state for a land allotment to be used for just such a garden, and he was granted 625 acres. There, he set about the task of creating a series of biblical landscapes.

Strictly translated, the name "Neot Kedumim" means "ancient pastures" (an alternative translation might be "ancient places of beauty"). When Nogah Hareuveni first came to the property, few names could have seemed so inappropriate. The land was barren, desolate, and deemed unfit for cultivation after centuries of abuse and overgrazing. Besides drawing on the botanical training he had received from his gifted parents, Hareuveni recruited the assistance of like-minded botanists and agronomists, with whom he began the slow process of reclaiming the land for cultivation.

Within the world of ecology, the success he achieved in bringing such damaged land back to fertility would be enough to earn Hareuveni accolades. But the "reclamation ecology" he and his team pioneered was only a means to a much more important end. He was not, after all, interested in just creating a new patch of farmland. He wanted to bring the biblical landscape to life! So once he knew the land was ready, he began to scour the world for the plants that would one day fill his gardens.

Many of the plants mentioned in the Bible never grew in Israel, like the cedar tree (imported by Solomon from Lebanon). Having succeeded in bringing life back to barren earth, Hareuveni was now faced with the new challenge of creating new mini-ecologies that would support nonindigenous plants. Here, too, he and his team succeeded.

In designing Neot Kedumim, Hareuveni did not content himself with simply finding plant species and cultivating them in a series of plots, groves, and beds. Instead, he chose the much more challenging—and symbolically resonant—approach of dedicating whole sections of the park to biblically inspired themes. One garden is dedicated to the prophet Isaiah (Isaiah's Vineyard), in whose Old Testament verses mention is made of the oak and the terebinth. Isaiah's reference to these trees were not made just in passing, but also as symbolic references to other, more important points. Hareuveni's presentation of them in Isaiah's Vineyard strives to convey this extra, symbolic reference.

Consistent with the overall philosophy of re-creating the symbolic meaning of the flora (and fauna) mentioned in the Bible, Hareuveni does not stop with aesthetically arranging his botanical exhibits. He takes everything a step further, incorporating the techniques of sowing and reaping and of threshing and preserving, to the annual harvest of crops included in the botanical reserve. He even goes so far as to keep on the reserve flocks of the breeds of sheep and goats and re-creates their biblically appropriate grazing fodder. Hareuveni's accomplishment is unique in the world—there are many biblical gardens, featuring plants mentioned in the Bible, but there is only one true landscape reserve, Neot Kedumim, where not just the botany, but equally important, the symbolism, is made manifest in all its inspirational glory. Little wonder, then, that thousands of Christians visit the reserve every year.

Via Dolorosa

In all the world, there is no stretch of roadway more profoundly moving and spiritually significant than the *Via Dolorosa* (Way of Sorrow, also called *Via Crucis*, or "Way of the Cross") in Jerusalem. It is the path that Jesus walked on the last day of His life, bearing on His own back the cross on which He would be crucified. For all Christians, throughout the world, this pathway is the start of the most inspirational event in the history of the world. When Jesus took His first step onto these streets, He set in motion not only His personal sacrifice but also the salvation of all humankind.

The Via Dolorosa began with Pilate's condemnation of Jesus in his Praetorium (Judgment Hall). From there, Jesus was forced out in the company of guards, who whipped Him and forced Him to carry the cross. He was forced to bear this burden as He walked through jeering crowds to the place of execution, a hill outside of town known by the name Golgotha. The route is only a half-mile in length, walked by modern pilgrims with ease in an hour or so. For Jesus, it must have seemed far longer.

The streets on which Jesus actually walked that long, terrible journey no longer exist. Jerusalem is an ancient city, and over the millenia, old streets were repaved and new buildings were constructed. To find the stones on which Jesus's feet actually trod, you would have to dig fifteen feet down from the street surface of today. Still, it isn't the cobblestones that matter—for pilgrims, the important thing is to follow the path and, in so commemorating the suffering of our Lord, to gain in spirit and express their faith.

The tradition of the Via Dolorosa was not a part of early Christian worship, although they knew well the passion and sacrifice that Jesus endured. It wasn't until sometime in the thirteenth century that the church first established what Catholics and some Protestant denominations refer to as the "Stations of the Cross," stages along Christ's way from His sentencing to death by Pilate to His execution on the hill of Golgotha. At first, there were more than thirty stations, each representing an incident in Christ's passion, for which a devout Christian was encouraged to devote at least a moment of reflection. While most of these stations were based on specific events mentioned in the Bible, several were based on legend instead. By the end of the fourteenth century, the church had eliminated many of the more spurious events, bringing the number of stations to fourteen, and that is what we retain today.

Along the route designated via Dolorosa in Jerusalem, a person wishing to walk Jesus's last road begins in the old city, at Pilate's Judgment Hall. From there he or she moves to a monastery that has been built on the site where Jesus is believed to have been scourged by Roman soldiers and forced to take up His cross. Both of these first stages of the journey are attested to by biblical reference. The next stop along the route is a chapel that was built by Polish soldiers sometime after World War II that is said to mark the spot where Jesus fell for the first time on His final journey. There is no biblical reference for this fall, however. Similarly unmentioned in the Bible, but part of a long-standing tradition, the next stage marks the place where Mary is said to have emerged from the crowd of jeering onlookers to make her presence known to Jesus. The fifth stop along the route marks the place where Matthew says an onlooker (Simon of Cyrene) was ordered to pick up Jesus's cross and bear it for a while.

The sixth stage of the via Dolorosa represents another event that has no biblical reference, but is much beloved in tradition. It is where a woman named Veronica broke free from the crowd to wipe the sweat and blood from Jesus's brow. The cloth she used, known today as the Shroud of Turin, is said to preserve the image of Christ's face, but this is the subject of much controversy. Stage seven is similarly unmentioned in the Gospels and marks the place where Jesus is said once again to have stumbled under His burden. The eighth station marks the place where, according to Luke 23:28, Jesus roused Himself from His own suffering and spoke to the women of Jerusalem. The ninth station marks another event that exists only in tradition but goes unmentioned in the Bible, in which Jesus falters under His burden for the final time.

The remaining five events commemorated by the via Dolorosa all occurred at the foot of the cross. The first is when the Roman soldiers stripped Jesus of His clothes. The second is the driving of the nails into Jesus's hands and feet. The third is Jesus's agony and death. The fourth marks the point where Jesus's followers claimed His body and prepared it for burial. The fifth, and final, is the actual burial of Jesus's body in a tomb provided by Joseph of Arimathea. All these events are attested to in the Gospels. For centuries, these final stages were all conducted in the Church of the Holy Sepulcher, built by Constantine in 326 B.C. In the 1800s, however, a Lutheran pastor questioned the validity of that location and chose another spot as being more likely to represent the actual location of Golgotha. A tomb, Gordon's Calvary and Garden Tomb, is built on this site, and it is favored by many Protestant visitors who walk the Way of the Cross.

VIII

HAPPY HOLIDAYS

From Christmas cheer to the Fourth of July, we take time out to celebrate our Christian heritage. Sometimes, our celebrations commemorate specifically religious occasions, notably Christmas and Easter, but because Christianity is so closely intertwined with American public life, our patriotic holidays also often hold a powerfully felt religious component.

Such celebrations provide Christians an opportunity to reflect on the importance of their faith. They also allow us to bear public witness to the beneficence of God and to express our joy at the salvation offered to all humankind by Jesus's sacrifice on the cross. They remind us of the reliance our ancestors placed on divine providence and present us with the opportunity to pass along the teachings of our faith to others.

Christmas

The centerpiece of the Christian holiday calendar is Christmas, when we celebrate the birth of Christ and the promise of salvation that His coming brought to all of humankind. Although it can sometimes seem as if commercialism has overshadowed the religious import of this holiday, a closer look at the way in which Christmas is celebrated by families and communities is reassuring. For most, the fellowship of friends and family gathered around the table for the Christmas feast far outweighs the frantic scramble for gifts under the tree. For most, it is also a time of spiritual renewal, when we join with our church community to hear again the Gospel of hope preached from pulpits across the nation.

Our Christmas holiday traditions have developed over the long centuries since Jesus first was born to open the way to salvation. At the heart of all Christmas celebrations is the depiction or reenactment of the nativity. Even in the modern secular environment, the representation of Christ sleeping peacefully in a Bethlehem manger, with Joseph and Mary looking on and the Magi offering their gifts, is still found on church lawns and in private homes. We reinforce this visual imagery with our tradition of attending Christmas worship, where the story of Jesus's birth is related and hymns celebrating His coming are customarily sung.

Many of our Christmas traditions are not specifically linked to biblical passages or practices handed down from the time of Jesus. Nonetheless, they have been a part of our holiday season for so long that they have taken on great symbolic importance. For instance, the Christmas feast, shared by friends and family, bears little resemblance to anything that Jesus would have known. Most American households offer either a Christmas ham (unacceptable in the Judaic tradition into which Jesus was born) or a turkey, whose natural habitat is limited to the New World. Still, the family gathering around the table reenacts values of fellowship and family unity that Jesus would undoubtedly recognize.

The most important physical icons of Christmastime in America are the gaily decorated tree and sparkling lights festooning our doors and windows. The tree, which stands ever green, even in the dead of winter, symbolizes new life and thus the birth of Jesus. The gifts beneath the tree represent the gifts borne by the Magi to present to the newborn Savior. The sparkling lights on the tree itself symbolize the starry sky, over Bethlehem, and the star at the very top is the North Star that guided the Magi to the manger where Jesus lay. The lights (often replaced by candles) that decorate our windows and doors express our openness to Christian spirit and our welcome of this most holy of seasons.

Easter

Easter is among the oldest of Christianity's holiday traditions. It is the day on which we celebrate the fulfillment of Christ's mission on earth and His resurrection from the dead. Its earliest celebrants had no set day on which to celebrate, but once the emperor Constantine converted to Christianity, he set himself the task of regularizing a number of church practices. It is Constantine who established the official date. He ruled that Easter should be celebrated once every year, on the first Sunday after the first full moon that followed the Vernal (spring) Equinox. The spring equinox marks the time when hours of daylight and dark are most nearly equal, and falls on March 20 or 21 in most years. The equinoxes were frequently used in ancient times as reference points to set important dates.

The Easter Sunday church service is an attempt to carry on the traditions set by the early church and marks the joyous news that "He is risen!" However, the entire Easter season also contains many other important events in the final days of Jesus's life. Palm Sunday, which occurs forty-six days before Easter, marks the day that Jesus entered Jerusalem for the final time. By now, His fame had spread, and people began to crowd around Him. They followed the local custom for welcoming the arrival of a great personage by throwing palms at the feet of His donkey to cushion His ride. Today, many denominations distribute palms to the congregation in memory of this event. Palm Sunday marks the beginning of Lent, traditionally a time of fasting among many Christian groups.

Ash Wednesday follows Palm Sunday. On this day, Christians of certain denominations (including Catholics, Episcopalians, and Lutherans) bring the palms received on Palm Sunday back to church to be burned. The priest or minister then daubs a little of the ash on the worshipper's forehead, where it should remain for the rest of the day as a visible mark of penitence.

Good Friday occurs immediately before Easter Sunday and commemorates Jesus's suffering and death on the cross. Many churches hold special services on this day, and most schools and businesses have traditionally closed early to allow people to go home and meditate on the passion of Jesus during this time.

Many folk traditions and symbols that have no grounding in early Christian practices have been added to the celebration of Easter Sunday today. The eating of eggs is believed to be a way to mark the end of

Lenten fasting. Decorating the eggs, however, is believed to have been adopted from Egyptian or Persian traditions. The Easter bunny beloved by so many children is another symbol most likely borrowed from Egypt, where the animal was believed to be a symbol of rebirth and renewal.

Independence Day

It may seem odd to include this or any other patriotic holiday in a book celebrating Christian traditions, but the choice is quite deliberate. Although the United States acknowledges no official religion, the fact remains that its first settlers were decidedly religious and devoted to creating a haven for their Protestantism, which was so unwelcome in Europe. Furthermore, the principles and traditions that guided these settlers were of paramount importance in shaping the thinking of the nation's founding fathers and the justifications they offered for their determination to secure independence were, also, profoundly informed by their faith.

It is in recognition of these facts that many American Christians approach the Fourth of July, our Independence Day, as a time to celebrate the history and traditions of their faith—for faith and love of country are so closely intertwined. When we watch the parade pass by along the streets of our towns, we see that intermingling of faith and patriotism clearly, for in most communities the marchers include members of our local church societies and fellowship organizations. When we take the family to view the fireworks in the evening, we are reminded of the words of our national anthem, which unashamedly affirms, "In God is our trust."

Independence Day is thus only superficially a secular holiday. It marks our nation's formal break with British rule, but it means a great deal more as well. The thoughtful among us will also use the day to reflect on the fact that our Revolution marks the *second* blow struck for freedom by the American colonists. The first was struck with the arrival of the Plymouth colonists, who dreamed of establishing a society truly committed to the teachings of the Christian scriptures.

We tend to lose sight of these truths when we get bogged down in controversies over the separation of church and state. A little reflection while under the inspirational influence of our local celebrations might help us move away from that contentiousness. It might help us to recall just why it was that our founders added that article to the Declaration of Independence. They remembered too well the persecutions endured by Reformation leaders in a home country whose ruler was also the autocratic head of a monopolistic state church. Their goal was not to wipe out all religious expression in the public sphere, but to guarantee that the religious sentiment of all kinds would forever be freely expressed.

Memorial Day

During the Civil War years, the nation was grievously divided, but on both sides one thing was shared: grief at the loss of the young men who had gone off to fight and die. From the beginning of the war's bloodshed, families in nearly every community across the North and South began the sad duty of burying their dead. In some areas, women's groups—primarily church based—also began the practice of laying flowers on every soldier's grave. There was nothing official about their actions—they were moved to do this out of a privately felt need to commemorate the dead and out of a sense of Christian duty to honor the sacrifice made by so many young men.

These private ceremonies were not organized across the nation, but occurred spontaneously instead. But no matter whether the site of commemoration was a cemetery in upstate New York or a single lonely grave in a southern town, the way in which the dead were honored was the same: flowers and wreaths left at gravesites with a moment of prayer to follow.

After the war, when the true cost in lives was finally recognized, many communities decided to follow the example of these church groups and instituted local, officially recognized days of prayer and reflection to honor the war dead and to use the day to pray for national reconciliation. Several asked their government representatives to take the commemoration one step further into established tradition, among them, the town of Waterloo, New York. In 1868, a local pharmacist with strong ties to his church wrote a letter to General John Logan, the commander of the Grand Army of the Republic. In response, on May 5, 1868, General Logan issued a proclamation declaring a national day of memorial and reconciliation while officiating at the interment ceremonies of both Union and Confederate soldiers in Arlington National Cemetery.

For the next five years, individual communities gathered on that day to remember their lost young men, but in 1873 the governor of New York signed into law the first statewide recognition of May 30 as Memorial Day. In 1890, the national government followed New York's lead, and the rest of the northern states soon followed suit, but the southern states each maintained their own traditional dates of commemoration. It was not until 1915, when the federal government extended the meaning of Memorial Day to cover all the nation's war dead that the holiday was recognized in the South as well. Even so, several southern states (Texas, Florida, Mississippi, Georgia, South Carolina, Louisiana, and Tennessee) still held separate Memorial Day observances specifically dedicated to their Civil War dead as well.

As befits a solemn day of mourning, the activities associated with Memorial Day have traditionally been restrained. Most communities came together to watch a solemn parade of veterans, then went with their families or church groups to the cemetery to lay wreaths and flags. Still central to the Memorial Day tradition was that quiet moment of reflection at the graveside. In 1922, however, a poem composed by the Canadian Lieutenant Colonel John McCrae was published as part of that year's Memorial Day observances. The poem, "In Flanders Field," recounts his impression of the vast cemetery of World War I soldiers who died in the Battle of Ypres.

The haunting opening lines of the poem ("In Flanders Field the poppies grow /Between the crosses, row on row") inspired an American woman, Moina Michaels, to compose her own response. In her poem, she singled out the image of the poppies, making it stand for the bloodshed and valor displayed by the soldiers who give their lives in war. Her verses inspired a French woman to begin making artificial poppies for sale, with the proceeds being used to provide for poor women and children who were widowed or orphaned during the war. In the United States, a similar project was begun to benefit wounded war veterans.

In 1951, the practice of laying flags on soldiers' graves was adopted by the Boy Scouts of America. At Arlington National Cemetery, this is the task of a special military unit, which also patrols the cemetery afterward to ensure that the flags remain in place. Over time, however, and particularly during the turbulent antiwar years of the 1970s, participation in traditional Memorial Day events diminished. Some also attribute this trend to the government's decision, in 1971, to move the holiday from its traditional date to "the last Monday in May." Critics argue that this change has made Memorial Day just one more long holiday weekend and has obscured its solemn meaning.

In 2000, Congress passed legislation declaring a national "moment of remembrance" at 3:00 P.M., local time, when all Americans are asked to set aside whatever they are doing and reflect on the meaning of sacrifice. After the tragic events of September 11, 2001, and the mobilization of American troops for war in Afghanistan and Iraq, the holiday has taken on renewed meaning in communities throughout the nation.

Seasons of Celebration

In addition to the established holidays, the Christian tradition recognizes a set of important times of the year that extend for several days or even weeks. They mark important events in the life of Jesus and are times of reflection and recommitment of faith. Some have celebratory traditions attached, but others often go unmarked except in church services and private reflection.

One of the best known of these seasons of celebration is Advent. This is the four-week period that immediately precedes Christmas Day. During this time, we commemorate the marriage of Joseph of Bethlehem to Mary of Nazareth, the announcement of Jesus's coming by the Holy Spirit, and the trek the young couple made to Bethlehem. Many households with children incorporate the Advent season in their Christmas traditions by keeping an Advent Calendar. Each day a child may open one of the many "windows" on the calendar to read a lesson on the coming of Christ's birth and be rewarded by a candy treat. Just as Advent precedes Christmas, the festival of Christmastide follows it. This season marks the time between Jesus's birth and the arrival of the Wise Men, from December 26 to January 6. In many families, January 6 is known as "little Christmas," and it is formally recognized on many church calendars as Epiphany.

The feast of the Epiphany marks the end of the Christmas season and the beginning of the Epiphany season. During this time, which lasts until Ash Wednesday, we celebrate Christ's years of teaching on earth. Toward the end of the season is Palm Sunday, marking Jesus's last public appearance before His death. The season ends on Ash Wednesday, when Lent begins.

Many Christian denominations mark Lent, a forty-day period of repentance, by embarking on a limited or symbolic fast. It is a time for personal reflection on how well we are living up to the challenge of maintaining Christian values. Many churches offer extra services during this period, to encourage their congregations to renew their commitment to Christ. Lent ends with the start of Holy Week, which leads up to Easter Sunday.

After Easter comes Eastertide, a celebration of the resurrection of Jesus and an expression of gratitude for the church He bequeathed to us. It lasts fifty days and is followed by the season of Pentecost, which commemorates the gifts of the Holy Spirit. It extends from the end of Eastertide to the beginning of Advent.

Thanksgiving Day

Thanksgiving is a specifically American holiday, not recognized anywhere else in the world. It has its roots in the earliest days of colonial settlement, and although it is not generally recognized as a religious feast day, it is nonetheless steeped in the Christian heritage handed down to us by our forefathers.

In November 1620, a hardy band of Pilgrims landed at Plymouth, on the coast of modern-day Massachusetts, to begin a new life in a new land. As staunch Christians who were fleeing religious persecution in England, they chose to trust in the Lord to help them build a society founded on biblical principles. These first settlers arrived just in time to face a harsh winter, and many died in the early months of the new settlement. When springtime arrived, the much reduced colony took stock of their situation, prayed for inspiration and help, and bravely planted their first crops. They trusted in the Lord to see them through.

As farmers, they knew that they were in a precarious position. Their survival depended on their harvest, without which they would never survive another winter. They put their hands to work in the fields and trained their eyes and hearts on Heaven, knowing that only God could protect their fields from harm. When harvest time came, they reaped their crops with joy, filling their storehouses with the food and seeds that guaranteed the life of their colony for another year.

A devout community of Christians, the Pilgrims knew that the harvest was not the result of their labors alone, but was rather the gift of divine Providence. They therefore set aside their labors once the harvest was done and declared a day of prayer and thanksgiving to the Lord. The celebration of the harvest and the giving of thanks to God became a regular annual event in the colony from that year onward.

Although our schoolchildren are taught that the first Thanksgiving feast also included a delegation of Indians, in honor of the help that these indigenous peoples gave to the early settlers, there is some dispute that this really happened. It is true that the colony traded with the local peoples from time to time and at times offered hospitality to visiting Indian traders with a feast, but these events were not necessarily a part of the annual harvest celebration. Today's story of a Thanksgiving fellowship between settlers and Indians had its beginnings in the early nineteenth century, in a story by Alexander Young that combined historical fact with a large measure of creative fiction.

Thanksgiving Day only achieved national status in 1781, when President George Washington called for a national day of unity, on which all Americans might remember the Lord and give Him our thanks. Washington thus linked the tradition of the early Pilgrim settlers with the formation of the newly independent nation. He set aside the date of November 26 as the official day of celebration. Before his edict, communities celebrating Thanksgiving did so on days of their own choosing. Other presidents have also declared days of prayer and thanksgiving to commemorate milestones in the nation's history, but none of these other dates were linked by tradition or intent to the original celebration held in Plymouth Colony.

Even with President Washington's declaration, there was no legislation conferring to Thanksgiving Day the status of a national holiday. Beginning in 1823, however, Sara Josepha Hale, who edited several widely read women's magazines of the day, began a campaign to change this situation. It took her forty years of editorializing and even personally badgering members of Congress, but she finally achieved her aim in 1863, when President Abraham Lincoln officially proclaimed the last Thursday in November as our national day of thanksgiving. In 1941, Congress finally got around to writing the national holiday into law.

Our traditions of Thanksgiving, from the turkey we eat to the decorations of dried corncobs and cornucopias, may seem to have no basis in Christianity in any scriptural sense. However, they are consistent with the Bible's tendency to celebrate the simple elements of life rather than elaborate ritual. The relevance of these symbols comes from their ability to remind us of the inspiration of that first harvest, when the Pilgrims humbly and sincerely took time out of their difficult lives to give praise and thanks to God for having seen them through hardship.

Valentine's Day

Valentine's Day is, today, a lighthearted holiday celebrated by children and romantic couples, in personal, often casual ways. Originally, however, it was a much more significant religious feast day, commemorating the martyrdom of an early Christian who lived during the years when Rome actively persecuted the followers of Jesus.

In the annals of the early church, the name Valentine (Valentinius) appears several times, so there are several men who might possibly have been the inspiration for the holiday. Only one, however, has a life story that seems consistent with what the holiday has come to mean in our traditions. This particular Valentine lived in Rome in the middle of the third century. He was a practicing Christian to whom many couples came for the performance of the ceremony that would sanction their marriage in the church.

During this time, in the years between 200 and 300, Rome was engaged in battles throughout the imperial territories. The emperor needed a constant, massive supply of young men to fill the ranks of his army. He decided that it best suited his purposes for the soldiers to be unmarried, because married men would constantly be thinking of their wives back home and would be more likely to desert the ranks to return to domestic life. He decreed that it would henceforth be illegal for soldiers to marry, and set grave penalties for any who were caught violating this new law.

Valentine was a firm believer in the biblical injunction for young men and women to marry. In violation of imperial law, he continued to counsel young couples to marry and to perform the appropriate marriage ceremonies whenever asked. But the emperor's spies were everywhere in Rome, and Valentine was inevitably caught. He was arrested and brought to trial, where he was sentenced to death. Imperial records show that he was executed on February 14, 269.

Valentine's commitment to the sanctity of marriage and his willingness to die in the furtherance of God's law would, in itself, be enough to recommend him for commemoration with a day dedicated to romantic love. But there is more to his story, and these further details are credited by many as the basis for our best-known Valentine's Day tradition: the exchanging of love notes.

While Valentine languished in prison awaiting the date of his execution, it is said that he began to receive visits from the daughter of his jailor. The two fell in love, even though there was no possibility that they would ever be permitted a life together. Every day he wrote her letters of love, which he signed with the simple words "Your Valentine." Today, the little cards our children exchange with one another—

Valentines—get their name from those long ago letters sent by a doomed prisoner to his beloved.

We have a later Roman emperor to thank for taking this delightful, if sad, story out of obscurity. In 313, the emperor Constantine converted to Christianity and made it the official religion of the state. This was the beginning of the officially constituted church. Under Constantine's urgings, the religious hierarchy set about ending the pagan religious ceremonies and festivals that had for so long been practiced in the empire. Church leaders realized that this could be an opportunity to do more than merely end pagan activities—it could also be an occasion by which to attract new converts to Christianity. Thus, instead of simply banning the pagan festivals, they replaced them with holidays commemorating Christian martyrs and celebrating Christian principles.

In the pagan calendar, the month of February was devoted to a festival called the Lupercalia, which honored the Roman Goddess Juno. The festival encouraged excess in drinking and in sexual licentiousness, and was therefore greatly disapproved of by the Christian church. It was banned in 496 and in its place the church proclaimed Saint Valentine's Day, thereby replacing pagan hedonism with a holiday honoring the sanctity of marriage.

Although Valentine's love letters from prison are believed to be the inspiration for the notes we exchange today, the practice did not become widespread in early Rome. It began in the Middle Ages, when Charles, the French duke of Orleans, was captured by the English and imprisoned following the Battle of Agincourt. From his lonely prison cell in the Tower of London, the duke emulated Valentine by sending love letters to his wife in France. These letters are believed to be the first true Valentine notes ever sent.

From the Middle Ages to the 1800s, Valentine cards were handmade and were mostly sent by romantic couples of the upper classes. The common folk marked the date with the exchange of less costly gifts, including hand-carved spoons bearing the image of a heart or a key, or presented one another with wildflowers. In 1840, Esther Howland got the idea to mass-produce Valentines and offer them for sale, and the public responded enthusiastically. Her first printing of 5,000 cards were sold out nearly overnight.

IX

MODELS OF MODERN CHRISTIANITY

The story of Jesus is dear to the hearts of all His faithful followers. His life and lessons provided the blueprint on which others attempted to pattern their lives. In the past two centuries, many of our most inspirational public figures and national leaders have been people of profound faith. Whether they acted as public servants, as leaders of social movements, or as religious spokespersons, they have led us all by their example and made extraordinary contributions to the nation's Christian heritage.

Dr. Norman Vincent Peale

Norman Vincent Peale, one of the most inspirational leaders this country has ever known, was born on May 31, 1898, in Bowersville, Ohio. He attended Wesleyan University, after which he was ordained in the Methodist Episcopal Church (1922). Over the next ten years he served as pastor to Methodist churches in Rhode Island and New York, but in 1932 he was invited to take over the ministry of Marble Collegiate Church in New York City. To accept this posting, he had to switch church affiliations to the Dutch Reformed denomination. Marble Collegiate would remain his base for the next fifty-two years.

Dr. Peale proved to be a highly effective preacher, and his sermons were distinguished by his emphasis on optimism. People flocked to his church to hear his positive message. He soon came to believe that there might be a wider audience for his optimistic ministry and, with his wife, Ruth Stafford Peale, he founded *Guideposts Magazine* in 1945. Like his sermons, the articles featured in this publication were upbeat, inspirational, and inclusive. He invited his readers, many of whom were celebrated public figures, to contribute their own inspirational stories for publication. His recipe of optimism and uplifting testimony made his magazine a great success, and even today it boasts a circulation in excess of 4 million readers.

In 1947, Dr. Peale joined forces with the educator Kenneth Beebe to bring his positive message to an even broader audience. Together, they founded the Horatio Alger Association, named after the unflaggingly optimistic hero of a popular early twentieth-century boy's book series. The primary function of the association was to seek out and reward Americans who, through positivism and hard work, conquered adversity and achieved success.

By now, Dr. Peale had become something of a household name, and at the age of fifty-four he was invited to write a book on his beliefs. The book, *The Power of Positive Thinking*, was published in 1952 and immediately leaped to the top of the national best-seller lists. Over the years, 20 million copies have been sold, and it has been translated into forty-one languages. His book has become a classic in the genre of inspirational literature. He went on to write more than forty other inspirational titles, but none ever achieved the international success of his first.

Early in his Marble Collegiate Church ministry, Dr. Peale began the practice of broadcasting his sermons on a weekly radio show called *The Art of Living*. Listeners were invited to ask for printed transcripts of the broadcasts, and it is reported that more than 750,000 such requests were honored every month. With the coming of television, he moved his on-air ministry to that new medium, eventually reaching the homes of millions of Americans. He remained active as a writer and preacher until his death on December 24, 1993.

At the heart of Dr. Peale's teaching was the belief that individuals are not at the mercy of an uncaring, impersonal fate. He believed that each of us has the God-given ability to turn aside adversity and overcome obstacles by hard work and by maintaining a positive attitude toward life. He believed that people can take greater control over their lives by the way they approach the world. Even a half-century after the first publication of his book, this message still strikes a resounding chord among millions of readers.

Dr. Martin Luther King Jr.

Martin Luther King Jr. was born in Atlanta, Georgia, on January 15, 1929. His father was a Baptist minister, as had been his grandfather. His great-grandparents had been sharecroppers. King attended local schools, then enrolled in Morehouse College, where he earned a degree in sociology in 1948. He was ordained a minister in the Ebenezer Baptist Church—the church of his father and grandfather—in that same year.

King next moved north to Pennsylvania to study at Crozer Theological Seminary, which granted him his BA in Divinity in 1951. He completed his education at Boston College, where he earned his doctorate in theology in 1955. He returned to the South to serve as pastor at the Dexter Avenue Baptist Church in Montgomery, Alabama, where he stayed until 1959. In his first year there, he was drawn into the civil rights movement that would shape the rest of his life.

Dr. King's theological training had opened him to the concept of activist ministry, as exemplified by early Protestant abolitionists and, from a very different culture, Mohandas Gandhi's doctrine of non-violent protest. When, in 1955, the Montgomery bus boycott was sparked by Rosa Parks, Dr. King was quick to see that this was an opportunity to put his beliefs into practice. He founded the Southern Christian Leadership Conference in 1957, through which he became intensely involved in the civil rights struggle, and ultimately resigned his position at the Dexter Avenue Baptist Church in 1959 to work full time in this cause.

Over the next decade, Dr. King devoted his considerable energies to fighting against racial segregation and discrimination, leading protest marches and giving inspirational speeches throughout the South and to sympathetic audiences in the North. In 1963, he catapulted to the nation's awareness when he delivered his most famous speech, "I Have a Dream." In this address, he invoked the guiding principles of his Christian faith and the premises on which this nation was founded, arguing that together they would one day lead to a society in which all men were truly created equal.

Largely through Dr. King's efforts, but with the assistance of many other organizations, large and small, Congress was moved to draft the Civil Rights Act of 1964, legally ending segregation and discrimination on the basis of race in this country. For his efforts, he was awarded the

1964 Nobel Peace Prize. He continued to work to ease racial divisions for the few years remaining to him. He was assassinated on April 4, 1968, by James Earl Ray. The fatal shot found its mark while Dr. King was waving to an admiring crowd from a hotel balcony in Memphis, Tennessee.

Pat Robertson

A controversial figure even in evangelical Christian circles, Pat Robertson has nonetheless made unique contributions to the role of faith in American public life. Born in Lexington, Virginia, on March 22, 1930, he grew up with a firsthand view of political life. His father, A. Willis Robertson, was a conservative congressman and, later, senator for the state of Virginia.

After earning his undergraduate degree and serving in the armed forces in Korea, Robertson enrolled in Yale Law School to earn his law degree. There, he met and married Adela Elmer in 1954. Always drawn to the faith, Robertson remained at Yale to study theology at the Divinity School and earned a master's degree in 1959.

Intrigued by the growing phenomenon of television and inspired by the early television ministries of Billy Graham and others, Robertson and his wife bought a defunct broadcasting station in Tidewater, Virginia, and created the Christian Broadcasting Network (CBN) in 1960. After a year of planning, the first broadcast of his on-air ministry was televised on October 1, 1961. He pioneered the use of the talk-show format, in which guests were invited to share their inspirational stories of faith. His program, which came to be called *The 700 Club*, gained a wide viewership, and is today one of the longest running evangelistic television programs.

Robertson's television presence, along with his fifteen books (including end-times–oriented fiction), brought him to a broader national awareness than most other evangelical leaders. His interest in and familiarity with the political sphere brought him the opportunity to serve on President Ronald Reagan's Task Force on Victims of Crime, to which he brought his strongly held conservative Christian perspective. By the middle of the 1980s, he was among the most well-known Christian spokespersons in the country, readily recognized even by much of the non-Christian population. By this time, he had added a number of other ministries to his CBN presence, including a pro-family media production company called International Family Entertainment.

In 1987, Robertson sought the Republican nomination for president, hoping to succeed Reagan in office. He resigned from his ministries to concentrate on his campaign and scored early successes in a number of primaries. His tendency to intemperance in his remarks scuttled his political chances, however, and some of his beliefs, particularly in faith-healing and prophesying, turned away some voters who otherwise supported his pro-life, pro-family platform. He dropped out of the race before the end of the primary season.

In the 1990s, Robertson returned to his original spheres of interest—the use of mass media and television in particular—to promote Christian values. He created the Family Channel cable network, which was devoted to showing only programs that the whole family could watch together. He also returned to hosting *The 700 Club*.

In 2000, he sold the Family Channel to focus his energies on public policy initiatives.

Ronald Reagan

Ronald Reagan, born on February 6, 1911, came to be affectionately known as "The Great Communicator." He was elected president in 1980, with the strong support of Christian communities throughout the nation. His pro-life, pro-family, pro-Israel stance resonated strongly with a populace that had grown weary of the apparent descent into hedonism, irresponsibility, and immorality of the last decades. In particular, voters from all parts of the political spectrum found the sincerity and simplicity of his Christian faith reassuring. He was, perhaps, the most widely loved and respected president to hold office in the modern era.

For Reagan, religious conviction came first from the example of his mother, Nelle. She took her responsibility to raise her child in the church seriously, insisting that he go to church every Sunday, promoting the study of the Bible, and exposing him to other inspirational literature. As a young man, he came across the book *That Printer of Udell's* (1903) by Harold Bell Wright, the author of evangelical novels. Reagan was so inspired by the book's message that, as soon as he finished reading, he went to his mother to announce his determination to declare his faith. Later in life he would have a similarly profound response to the Whittaker Chambers book, *Witness* (1952), which chronicled the author's spiritual awakening. The story of redemption told by Chambers, formerly an atheist and avowed communist, deeply influenced Reagan both in terms of his faith and in his ideological conviction of the evils of communism.

Reagan brought his essential optimism and commitment to the power of prayer to the Oval Office. Dismissing the politically correct trend against public prayer, he routinely opened his daily cabinet meetings with a moment of prayer—the first president to do so since Dwight D. Eisenhower. He frequently affirmed that biblical wisdom was indispensable to good governance and good law, and in his speeches to the nation he openly called for America's spiritual awakening, saying "freedom prospers only where the blessings of God are avidly sought and humbly accepted." With the support of Christian movements such as the Moral Majority, and with the endorsement of Christian leaders such as Billy Graham, he successfully ran for a second term of office. When the world learned in 1988 that he suffered from Alzheimer's disease, the outpouring of sympathy and prayer was momentous. He died on June 5, 2004, and leaders from around the world turned out to mark his passing with affection and great sorrow.

Jimmy Carter

While the nation has enjoyed the leadership offered by presidents of strong religious faith, it was only with the 1976 election of President Jimmy Carter that a self-proclaimed born-again, evangelist Christian ever reached the Oval Office. His aim in life has been to embody, as best he could, the principles of Christian faith and charity.

James Earl Carter Jr. was born in Plains, Georgia, on October 1, 1924. His parents, James Earl and Lillian Gordy Carter, were both members of the local Baptist church, and they raised all their children in that faith. James Sr. was a successful local businessman, owning warehouses, cotton gins, and a working peanut farm. He was active in local politics, and both he and Lillian encouraged their children to take active roles in civic life. It is perhaps to Lillian that we can trace the future president's commitment to activist Christianity—she was a strong opponent of segregation during the civil rights era and even joined the Peace Corps once her children were grown.

At the age of ten, Jimmy Carter underwent immersion baptism and says that he was "born-again" at this time. He graduated from the U.S. Naval College at Annapolis in 1946, and following graduation he married his childhood sweetheart, Rosalynn Smith. He served in the Navy as a submariner, but following his father's death in 1954 he returned to Plains to take charge of the family business. Once back home, he took the responsibilities of teaching Sunday school and serving as a church deacon—two roles he continues to fulfill today.

Carter began his political career with a successful run for the state senate in 1962. Four years later he made an unsuccessful bid for governor, but succeeded in his second try in 1970. His governing style was consistently driven by the conviction that moral righteousness, not political expediency, was the standard on which a political leader should base all decisions.

In 1976, Carter was elected to the U.S. presidency. He took office during a period of economic distress and political disarray, particularly in the wake of the scandals that plagued the Richard Nixon presidency. His term in office was criticized by both liberals and conservatives, and he was unable to gain the cooperation of Congress to enact many of the policies he held dear. He ran for a second term, but lost to the Republican candidate, Ronald Reagan.

Once he was out of office, Carter found more understanding from his former critics. Most came to recognize that, even if they disagreed with his specific policy initiatives or political style, they could appreciate the sincerity of the moral values by which he was motivated. Outside of the pressures of Washington, Carter turned his energies to pursuing the goals he held most dear: to help the weak and the poor, to work for peace, and to bring comfort and healing to the sick. He established the Jimmy Carter Work Project of Habitat for Humanity, which constructs houses for the homeless. The movement has grown immensely since its inception in 1981, having built more than 100,000 homes in 60 countries. With his wife he also established the Carter Center, which combines a think tank on policy with the administration of practical projects designed to resolve human rights and health problems around the world. He has personally gone on missions of peace to war-torn regions of the world, including East Timor, Haiti, and the Middle East, to act as conflict mediator. His humanitarian efforts were recognized by the world in 2002, when he was awarded the Nobel Peace Prize.

Billy Graham

William Franklin Graham Jr. was born on November 7, 1918, in North Carolina, into a devout Presbyterian household. He was the first of four children born to William Franklin and Morrow Coffey Graham. At the age of one he was baptised into his parents church. He attended local schools but was uncertain what to do with his life, so he postponed college. At the age of twenty-six he attended a revival where the preacher, Mordecai Fowler Ham, made a powerful impression on him. He immediately decided that he had a call to ministry.

Graham enrolled in Bob Jones College in Tennessee in 1936, but transferred within a year to the Florida Bible Institute, where he studied theology. During this time he underwent immersion baptism to change his affiliation from Presbyterian to Southern Baptist. He also embarked on a mission of public preaching on street corners, in relief missions, and wherever else he could find an audience willing to listen.

Graham quickly became known as a gifted, inspirational speaker. One of his admirers helped him to attend Wheaton College, where he studied anthropology from 1940 to 1943. While still a student, he took the post of pastor at the nearby United Gospel Tabernacle. He also married Ruth Bell, the daughter of Presbyterian missionaries who had grown up in the missions in China and elsewhere in Asia.

At this time, Graham was casting about for an appropriate way to carry out his evangelical mission. He was drawn to the potential of radio broadcasting for reaching a wider public with his evangelical message. In 1944, he began his first radio ministry, but left it when he was invited to participate in a revivalist movement called Youth for Christ (YFC). With this group, he got his first real taste for the large-scale revivalist meetings that would later become his trademark. Although he was highly popular in the YFC, by 1948 he was ready to launch his own independent mission. He brought with him colleagues he had known from his first radio days and enlisted Grady Wilson, a boyhood friend, to serve as associate evangelist.

Graham's rallies were very popular, and he was soon drawing record crowds. He didn't achieve national fame, however, until 1949, when a notorious criminal and a local radio personality were moved to declare themselves for Christ at a rally in Los Angeles. The influential publisher William Randolph Hearst began publishing flattering articles and editorials about Graham's ministry. Soon after, Henry Luce, who published *Time* and *Life* magazines, did the same, and Graham became a household name.

With his newfound celebrity, Graham's rallies (which he called Crusades) now grew to vast proportions. He returned to radio, beginning with 150 stations. In time, 1,200 radio stations carried his broadcasts, bringing his message to tens of millions of listeners. He soon did the same thing on television, further expanding his mission.

In the late 1950s, Graham and his wife founded the Billy Graham Evangelistic Association (BGEA) to manage his many projects and interests. The BGEA oversaw the operation of a variety of media outlets, including World Wide Pictures (Christian-themed films) and Grason Company (book and magazine publishing). Graham also launched a television show called *Hour of Decision*, which ran from 1951 to 1954, and founded *Decision Magazine*. During this decade, he also became a confidant to President Dwight D. Eisenhower, the first of his presidential associations.

Graham still held his highly popular Crusades, which by 1959 were drawing hundreds of thousands of attendees. In 1962, he launched a series of seminars and continued to serve as the elder statesman of evangelistic Christianity to the powerful in Washington and in American industry. In the 1970s, his public image suffered somewhat because of his friendship with Richard Nixon, then embroiled in the Watergate scandals. Nonetheless, every American president has sought him out since Eisenhower, and George H. W. Bush has called him "America's pastor." He retired at the age of eighty-two in 2000, turning over the management of his ministry to his children.

X

ROOTS OF TRADITION

Christianity has undergone innumerable changes since the days when Jesus first went forth to carry His teachings into the broader world. It has endured and prospered through the time of persecution in early Rome, to the extraordinary explosion of reformist movements throughout Europe, to its unique relationship with the rise of the grand political experiment known as the United States. Contemplating the high points of this long journey of faith can only strengthen our commitment to the Christian tradition.

The Era of Persecution

The years between Jesus's crucifixion and 313 were dark for those who professed Christianity. In matters of faith, their lives were imbued with joy, but they were forced to celebrate that joy in secret, because the most powerful force on earth had set itself against them. That force was Imperial Rome, which demanded that its citizens worship pagan gods and condemned Christianity not only as heresy but also as treason. Thus, to openly profess one's faith in Jesus's teachings was certain to earn swift arrest, brief imprisonment, torture, and execution.

The Roman emperors of this era were, for the most part, single-minded in their determination to eradicate the Christians in their midst. Christians were blamed for everything that went wrong, from a poor harvest to storms. The most extreme of these accusations was charged in 64, when a great fire (possibly set by the emperor Nero himself) leveled much of the city of Rome. Christians were hunted down by the hundreds and put to death in a variety of grisly ways. Tacitus, a historian of the period, described crucifixions, but also spoke of Christians being used as human torches to light Nero's feasts and of prisoners forced to wear bloody animal hides and then thrust into a cage with wolves or other fierce beasts to be gnawed to death. Under Nero's reign, Paul was beheaded and Peter was crucified.

Later emperors never quite matched the evil ingenuity of Nero, but at least eight of them actively pursued the policy of arresting and executing Christians whenever they could be found. Christians were accused of everything from cannibalism to plotting to overthrow the empire, but there was never any evidence. One or two emperors of the period showed relative leniency, reducing the punishment for professing Christianity to simple confiscation of property and exile of the offenders and their families. This was the policy of the emperor Domitian, who ordered mass exiles from 90 to 96. Among those he exiled was the apostle John. Domitian did consider killing all surviving descendants of the House of David—Jesus's kin—but he relented at the last moment, deciding they were too poor and rustic to ever pose a threat to him.

In the end, some scholars have estimated that as many as 100,000 Christians were tortured and executed during the time of persecutions. Still, throughout the whole era, the church continued to grow and thrive. As Tacitus noted, they had a powerful advantage over the forces of Rome. After all, Roman soldiers were willing to kill for their emperor, but Christians were willing to die for their Lord.

Constantine's Conversion

When the emperor Constantine assumed the throne in Rome in 306, he was not a Christian. He was also not very secure in his rule, because he had a brother who wanted to depose him and take his place. For six years, the two battled for ultimate control, until a fateful battle was fought in 312. On the night before the battle, Constantine is said to have had a dream or vision of Jesus, in which he was told to mount the symbol of Christ (called the *Chi Rho*) on his banners. He did as he was told and rode off to victory the following day. He formally accepted Christianity in the following year.

Constantine was not a man of half-measures. When he converted to Christianity, he also appointed church elders to his cabinet of trusted advisors. In addition, he made Christianity the state religion, supplanting the previous worship of Sol Invictus (a sun god cult). He ordered the construction of churches throughout the empire, including several within the city of Rome. Among these was Saint Peter's Basilica, marking the place on Vatican Hill where that apostle had been crucified.

After Constantine moved the imperial capital to Byzantium, he sent his mother back to Bethlehem, where she oversaw the construction of the Church of the Nativity.

Constantine began an aggressive policy of persecution during his reign, but this time the targets were not Christians. Instead, he hunted out pagans, whom he ordered to be forcibly converted. He also grew watchful for dissension within the church against established policies and severely punished any dissenters (heretics) he found.

After Constantine's death in 337, there was a brief period when the future was uncertain for Christians in the empire. Some of his sons, all of whom were contending for the throne, were not sympathetic to the faith of their father. Soon, however, the anti-Christian brothers were eliminated from the succession, and the history of the rest of the Constantine dynasty is one of support for the church. It was also, however, a time of increasingly restrictive dogma and of brutal repression of dissenting theological opinion.

Reformation and Reaction

The watershed moment in the development of Christianity as we know it today occurred in 1517, when the German theologian and Catholic priest Martin Luther issued his bold challenge to the Catholic Church. He nailed a document, known as the "95 Theses," to the doors of Castle Church in Wittenberg.

Luther had many problems with the church as it had evolved over the centuries. He felt it had become corrupt and elitist, and that it had strayed too far from the teachings of its founder. Most of all, he was appalled at the practice of selling indulgences. The church had become hungry for money and found it expedient to permit its wealthier patrons to "buy" redemption by willing their estates to the church following their deaths. For Luther, this was an abomination—salvation was a matter for God alone to grant, through the intercession of Jesus. When the church would not listen to his protests, he broke with it and founded his own Christian movement.

Luther's actions were the boldest of that era, but he was not the only voice calling for reform. In England, there was a growing unrest within the clergy, particularly with regard to the fact that the common people were not allowed direct access to the Bible. A variety of reform-minded groups sprang up during the 1400s and 1500s, each inspired by the desire to return the church to the original teachings of Jesus. But by this time the established church was far more interested in preserving its power than in engaging in theological and procedural reform. Rather than enter into a dialog with the reformers, it punished them with arrest, exile, and even execution.

The groundswell of support for reform would not be turned back, however. The new reformist sects were attracting a great many adherents, thinning the congregations of the established church. In addition, since the church was intimately linked with the royal houses of Europe, these dissenting groups were seen as potentially disastrous for political stability. The church counterattacked with two main weapons: the Inquisition and the Society of Jesus, otherwise known as the Jesuits. The first was intended to quash reformist heresies. The second was sent forth to recruit new members for the church by going into the world to minister to the poor, educate the youth, and establish missions to convert pagans in far-off lands.

The Jesuits enjoyed a large measure of success, but the Inquisition was another matter entirely. It sponsored a brutal regime of terror and torture to force reformists and dissenters to recant and return to the established dogma of the Catholic Church. Many leaders in the Reform movement were, indeed, killed, but there were always new ones to rise up and carry on. Eventually, the Catholic hierarchy had to acknowledge defeat, and the Inquisition withered away in the early years of the seventeenth century, whereas the reformers, in the form of new Christian denominations, lived on.

The Pilgrim Experiment

The Pilgrims, officially called Separatists, were an offshoot of Calvinism that took an extreme stance against the established Church of England. Strictly speaking, they were not a reformist movement, because they had no desire to fix the errors in the state church's policies and dogma. Instead, they wanted to break completely free of outside control. Their beliefs put them in an impossible position in England—they would not compromise with the established church, even after Catholicism had been supplanted by Protestantism, and the established church could not allow them to refuse to compromise. By their intransigence, they were, by definition, outlaws.

The Separatists ultimately found that exile from England was the only answer. They went first to Holland, where they stayed for thirteen years, but in 1620 a group of them decided to make a brave experiment. They would sail to the New World to create a colony that conformed fully to the teachings of the Bible. To secure a ship and crew to take them on their journey, they were forced to enter into an agreement with some merchants: In return for passage, they would turn over all the goods that they grew, made, or found, other than what was needed for survival, for the first seven years of their colony.

In September 1620, 102 passengers boarded the *Mayflower*. Of these, only forty-one were Separatists—there were no others in the church who were willing to risk the journey. The rest of the passenger list was made up of "strangers," allowed to join the group solely to fill out the passenger list. They landed at Plymouth in November and immediately set about readying their little colony for the winter that was soon to come.

From the start, these settlers intended to organize their lives and their community according to biblically derived principles. All the adult men in the group, including the "strangers," signed the Mayflower Compact, which was the first constitutional document governing an American settlement. According to the agreement, they would elect their leaders, and the community would draw up their laws after a close consultation with scripture. This principle of elected government was one of their great contributions to the future American government.

There were great hardships to be faced, of course. During the first winter, sickness struck the colony, eventually killing half of the settlers. The colony made contact with local Indian tribes fairly early in their stay and established trade relations, which helped augment their meager provisions. In the spring, the survivors of the harsh winter planted their first crops. The colonists drew on the guidance of the Bible to order their relationship with the local tribes, but did not appear to engage much in evangelizing. They weathered further hardships, from poor harvests to a near outbreak to open hostilities with the natives, but by 1623 they were well established and the continued survival of their settlement was ensured.

Utopian Societies

In the eighteenth century, European and American churches were swept up in a "Great Awakening," during which revivalist organizations sprang up by the hundreds. It was a time of great optimism, in which many people joined millennarian movements. It seemed to many that the time of the second coming of Christ might be just around the corner. In this highly charged, emotional atmosphere, many of the new movements became convinced that they could create Heaven here on earth—utopia. The urge that motivated these groups is having a resurgence in America today, in some corners of Christendom, although it remains a movement on the margins of society. The signs are all perceived to be around, and belief in the coming apocalypse is reflected in the rise in "end-times" literature and the recent move by some Christian groups to withdraw from traffic in the "non-Christian" world.

Christian utopian societies (there were secular ones as well) depended on scripture to guide every aspect of their daily lives. Although some attempted to create their utopias within the larger, nonbelieving culture, they quickly recognized that, to fully live by this principle, they would have to withdraw from the secular world, and even from fellow Christians who did not share their utopian beliefs. Sometimes, the need to withdraw was due to persecution by outsiders who did not understand them, but more often it was because the constant bombardment of outside temptations too easily lured their members away.

Common to all utopian communities was a commitment to communal living and a philosophy that strongly valued manual labor. In many other areas of doctrine, however, they differed greatly from one another.

Most of these societies shared the general belief that, with the return of Christ imminent, they had to make a great effort to more closely follow his teachings. In fact, they felt that their very effort might hasten His arrival. One of the best known of these groups are the Shakers, officially named the United Believers in Christ's Second Coming. They were founded by Ann Lee, called Mother by her followers, in England in 1758. They moved to America in 1774 and established colonies in and around New England. By the time of the Civil War, the communities boasted an aggregate membership of more than 6,000 followers.

Shakers believed in strict separation of the sexes, to the point of lifetime celibacy. They could only grow their numbers through recruitment from outside their communities. They got their familiar name from their form of worship, which called on the Holy Spirit to descend into them—when that happened, they would fall into a type of shaking, dancing trance. They were also ardent abolitionists, harboring escaped slaves along the Underground Railroad. They began as farmers, but later became known for furniture making. The longest surviving Shaker settlement was in Enfield, New Hampshire. Several Shaker settlements are now National Historic Landmarks.

Another utopian society to come to the United States from Europe was the group known as the Rappites, after their founder, Johan Georg Rapp. Similar to the Shakers in many ways, including the emphasis on celibacy, the group came to Pennsylvania to establish several communities beginning in 1903. The group lasted until 1905, when it found increasing difficulty in recruiting members due to the rules regarding celibacy. It might have survived nonetheless by relying on outside recruitment, but dissension regarding theological points put an end to that hope. It dissolved in 1905.

The most famous American-born utopian society is the Oneida Community of upstate New York. It was founded in 1833 by John Humphreys Noyes, a Yale-trained theologian and abolitionist. Noyes's distinctive doctrine involved a belief in "attainable perfection" within our lifetime. His group was committed to what he called "Bible communism," in which all members were obliged to contribute their labor to the group. The community was financially very successful during the forty or more years that it existed. Its downfall was triggered by Noyes's doctrine of "complex marriage," whereby every member was considered married to every other member. This enraged the religious leaders in their neighboring communities, and the group's members were officially condemned from many local pulpits. The group broke up in 1879, and Noyes himself fled to Canada in that same year.

Evangelicals of Television

With the advent of radio in the late 1800s, it was only natural that evangelicals would take to the airwaves to spread their message of the Gospel. In short order, religious programming became a regular feature on radio stations, and hundreds of radio evangelists sermonized over the air. With the spreading popularity of television in American households in the 1950s, the attraction of the new medium also proved irresistible.

Billy Graham was one of the very first to get involved in this new medium, and one of the first to be successful at it. He routinely aired his popular Crusade revivals, but also inaugurated a regular weekly show in 1950. His high public profile guaranteed him a ready-made audience willing to tune in, and his powerful speaking style was guaranteed to keep them listening. He was soon joined on the air by other popular preachers, including Rex Humbard, Jerry Falwell, and Oral Roberts.

These early television evangelists faced a certain amount of opposition when they sought to purchase broadcast time on network television. Critics cited violations of church and state, but the Federal Communications Commission ruled in favor of the evangelists. They also faced criticism from others in the evangelical community, who accused the television evangelists of "diluting" their message in an effort to appeal to wider audiences. Nonetheless, television evangelism continued to prosper. At first, Graham led all others in ratings, but his association with President Richard Nixon hurt his image in the mid-1970s, which opened the way for Jimmy Swaggart to take the lead. Meanwhile, as Swaggart was making headway and Pat Robertson founded the first Christian station to buy its own broadcast satellite, James and Tammy Faye Bakker were steadily gaining an audience for their talk-show formatted *Praise the Lord* broadcast. Also during this time, new faces were lining up to try their hands at televangelizing.

In the 1980s, a series of high-profile scandals involving prominent televangelists made headlines. Allegations of misuse of donated monies by a handful nearly destroyed the credibility of all televangelists. To ward off such a fate, the National Religious Broadcasters Organization established an Ethics and Financial Integrity Commission to act in a watchdog capacity. Honest televangelists welcomed the move because they recognized it would help clear their names of any taint of scandal. While the number of televangelical ministries appearing on network and cable channels has dwindled from their heyday in the mid- and late 1970s, religious broadcasting remains strong and is currently experiencing a new period of growth.

Moral Majority

In the 1950s, the nation enjoyed a brief period of relative peace and calm. True, there were worries about the Soviet Union, and the cold war was already in full swing, but under the leadership of grandfatherly Dwight D. Eisenhower, the average citizen felt more or less secure. In the 1960s, all that changed, however. The civil rights movement rekindled old divisions that had slumbered, unnoticed by most, in the century since the Civil War. The rise of rock and roll made many parents decidedly uneasy. Protests against the Vietnam War and the onset of the "counterculture" added to the sense of social upheaval. It seemed like every tradition was being challenged or simply ignored.

Early in this era of social unrest, concerned conservatives drawn largely from Christian groups formed the New Right Movement, hoping to do something to bring things back under control. They sought to restore traditional values and lifeways that they believed were being threatened by activists who favored such things as the Equal Rights

Amendment (ERA), abortion rights, and other examples of what came to be called "secular humanism."

Among the early participants in this movement was an evangelical minister, Jerry Falwell. As the host of a popular radio program and one of the early television evangelists, he had something of a national presence. He was also powerfully committed to the belief that political activism was a biblically mandated duty of all faithful Christians. He advocated for the positions taken by the New Right, but even his high-profile advocacy did not make much headway against the social and political changes sweeping the nation during the 1960s and 1970s.

In 1979, however, Falwell saw his chance. The Republican Party was coalescing behind the presidential candidacy of Ronald Reagan, whose values and beliefs fit well with the Christian community. Falwell threw his support behind Reagan's candidacy and formed a political action association to further this cause. He called this new organization the Moral Majority, expressing his belief that most Americans longed for a return to Christian values but were unsure of how to bring it about.

Members of the Moral Majority became extremely active in politics, beginning with Reagan's election and continuing throughout his presidency. They wrote letters to newspapers, took out advocacy ads, lobbied government officials, and sought positions in the nation's policy think tanks, all in an effort to influence public policy. Their principle causes were the defeat of the ERA, the overturning of *Roe vs. Wade*, rolling back the gay rights movement, and returning prayer and biblically acceptable teachings such as creationism in public schools. They sought a change in the role of government, which they believed should be strong on defense, vigilant against communism, and economically neutral. Furthermore, they believed that the federal government had no place in the family sphere, including the education of children. The organization published a monthly newsletter, *The Minority Report*, which regularly reported on—and graded—the voting records of senators and representatives.

The exact membership figures for the Moral Majority have never been clear. Some 600,000 newsletter subscriptions have been claimed, but Falwell and other organization leaders have set their membership at much higher levels. Some have claimed that, at its peak, the organization boasted more than 3 million members. In 1989, however, the organization was dissolved, in part because of problems that began to arise within the ranks of the more public evangelical figures associated with it.

Although the movement had been dissolved, Falwell remained committed to political activism in the name of Christian values. He has said that the three duties of an evangelical are to "save souls, baptize, and get people registered to vote." Buoyed by the outcome of the 2004 elections, he has recently announced plans to revive the Moral Majority as a political action group with a new name: the Faith and Values Coalition.

Christian Coalition

Like the Moral Majority, the Christian Coalition represents a modern watershed in the ways that religious values can merge with political action. Founded in 1989 by Pat Robertson, it is headquartered in Chesapeake, Virginia. Its mission is to give Christians a broader voice in government and to advance a conservative Christian political agenda. It is also dedicated to training Christian leaders in effective political action, initiating and guiding grassroots action, and acting as a watchdog agency to keep track of congressional and senatorial votes. A primary function is to publish and distribute voter guides before every election in every community in which it has established a branch.

That adds up to a great many communities. The organization boasts some 1,500 branches spread across all 50 states and 1.7 million members. At the outset, Robertson took the helm, with pro-life activist Ralph Reed as his deputy.

The Christian Coalition campaigns tirelessly for its agenda. Among its most cherished goals is the reinstitution of school prayer, the dismantling of the welfare system, and the institution of a ban on abortions. It bemoans what it perceives to be the moral decay of the government and argues that the only solution is to elect candidates of proven Christian values.

Under Reed's leadership, the organization has put together a strategy of grassroots campaigns designed to help get acceptable candidates into local and state offices, but it has also grown to have a powerful voice in key national elections as well. The organization is credited with having been instrumental in the elections of more than 200 candidates to local, state, and national office. In response to allegations that the tax-exempt organization was violating electoral laws, the organization split into two separate agencies in 1999: the tax-exempt voter education division and the tax-liable political action side.

XI

SYMBOL AND RITUAL

The teachings of Christ, even when couched in parables, are clear. For this reason, they have weathered the centuries without diminishment. But as individuals, our experience of faith is immediate and direct, and it is far more difficult to find words that will let us share it with others. That is one reason why religious symbols become so important. Symbols allow us to share the emotional, subjective experience of faith when words alone cannot do the job. The same is true for ritual and ceremony. They help us move from a purely intellectual understanding, to a deeper realization based on experience.

Take, for instance, the concept of fellowship. We all know what the word means. But how much deeper is our understanding when we gather together with others during church services? Similarly, we can talk about Jesus's sacrifice for our sins, but how much more profoundly do we understand that sacrifice when we reenact His last supper at communion?

Symbols of Christianity, whether they take the form of physical things, like the crucifix, or are embodied in ritual acts, such as baptism, serve us in two ways. They strengthen our faith, by providing reminders of the abiding truths that Jesus taught. They also permit us to bear witness to those truths to the wider world. They are a way of offering up our praises to the Lord.

Baptism

The ritual of baptism lies at the heart of Christianity and marks a transition from the established practices of Judaism to the rise of the Christian church. It marks an individual's entry into the church, the renunciation of sin, and the acceptance of Jesus and His teachings. The word comes from the Greek and means "immersion" or "dipping."

In the Old Testament, the central rite of initiation was circumcision. Ritual cleansing by water was a regular practice, but it did not mark a believer's entry into the faith. Nonetheless, the Old Testament references no doubt informed John the Baptist in his decision to begin baptising in Jesus's name, as a way of showing renunciation of sin and entry into the life of the Spirit. For instance, Exodus 36:25 tells us, "I will sprinkle clean water on you, so you will be clean," and in Psalms 51:1-3 we read, "Wash away my iniquity and cleanse me from my sin." Old Testament mentionings of ritual cleansing imply that ritual was a symbolic act of purification in preparation for other holy rituals, such as marriage, but it did not take on the meanings assigned to it today until the coming of Jesus.

The first to baptise in the Christian sense was, of course, John the Baptist, who preached the imminent coming of the Lord on the shores of the Jordan River. He believed that the people needed to prepare themselves for this momentous coming by washing away their sins, and to do so he led believers, one by one, into the river waters to confess their faith before being fully immersed. When Jesus learned of John the Baptist's ministry, He, too, went to the river and, although He was without sin, submitted to the baptismal rite at John's hands. By doing so, He sanctified the practice and made it a part of His own teachings. However, He did not personally perform baptisms as a part of his ministry.

Baptism served several purposes. It marked a convert's entry into the church, so it was the primary rite of initiation. It opened the way to salvation, and in many churches (but not all) it is the single necessary rite to achieve that end. It provided the convert with his or her first public opportunity to profess him- or herself as a believer, and it washed away the mark of Adam and Eve's original sin.

According to the available historical records, the early church did not practice infant baptism, as is practiced by many Christian churches today. Some argue that the markings and inscriptions in the catacombs around Rome indicate that infants were baptised, but the evidence is ambiguous at best. The first specific mention of the practice of infant baptism does not occur until the late second century. Similarly, evidence of baptism by sprinkling or annointing does not appear in the

New Testament or in the writings of the earliest church members. Full immersion of adults was the accepted rule.

John the Baptist took his guidance from the Old Testament prophets. Their words foretold of the coming of God's Kingdom and stated that this coming would be preceded by the return of Jews to their homeland and their immersion in the cleansing waters of the Jordan River. His work, as he saw it, was to hasten that joyous day by performing that prophetically ordained cleansing.

In the New Testament, baptism is almost always mentioned in the context of belief. It fact, a period of instruction lasting as long as two to three years was prescribed, and just before the rite, the subject of the baptism was expected to fast for two or three days. Because of this, many church leaders during the Reformation rejected the established practice of baptising infants. They referred to Mark 16:16, "And he that believeth and is baptised shall be saved." Because the word *belief* precedes the word *baptised*, the idea of infant baptism is thought to be contradictory to biblical teaching—how can an infant possess the necessary understanding to believe?

This position was not uniformly held throughout the Reformed church, however. In fact, controversy about infant baptism and the rites associated with the general ritual were fundamental issues of contention during the Reformation. Many continued to accept the practice of the established church and permitted infant baptism and baptism by sprinkling and annointing. The Anabaptists (e.g., Amish, Hutterites, and Mennonites) and Calvinist Reformers had the strongest views on the subject. For both groups, infant baptising was without merit, and for the Baptists in particular, full immersion was the only acceptable form of the rite.

The terms of this debate center around the twin concepts of baptism: by water and by Spirit. For some, including the founder of the Baptist Church, John Smyth, baptism in the Spirit required the conscious acceptance of faith. John Calvin added an extra controversy to the mix. He believed strongly that salvation was possible through faith alone. Therefore, he argued, baptism was not necessary for salvation. In this opinion he stood nearly alone among the founders of the Reform churches. He did not argue that baptism should not be practiced—he recognized it as a rite instituted by God and sanctified by Jesus—but he saw it more as a mark of initiation and an opportunity to openly declare one's faith.

The Biblical Garden

The world of the Bible is far distant in space and time from our own, yet in the pages of scripture we are given a glimpse of that world. This is accomplished, in part, through the many descriptions of the places in which the people of the Bible lived. In both the Old and New Testaments, we are given descriptions of everyday life, of the landscapes through which our ancestors in Spirit once walked. The litany of plants mentioned in the Bible include some that sound exotic and fanciful to our ears, and others that strike us as old familiar friends: daisies and buttercups, mallow and hyssop.

For centuries, Christian gardeners have included the more familiar species of flowers and herbs in their plantings, but it has really only been during the last half of the twentieth century that horticulturalists have been able to identify many of the biblical plants with real certainty. This breakthrough in knowledge has inspired a new symbolic art form practiced by many Christian churches: the planting of special, themed gardens that feature the plants mentioned in the Bible.

Some biblical gardens are simple affairs, but others, like the Warsaw Biblical Garden in Warsaw, Indiana, are quite extensive. Many feature different, themed areas commemorating a particular book or even verse of the Bible, others attempt to re-create different types of biblical landscapes: deserts, vinyards, and the like. What is of deepest importance to the crafters of the garden is that the plants chosen for display are of the actual genus and species of the plants of biblical times.

For many churches, the creation of the garden is an affair in which the entire congregation is welcome to participate. Some, like the First Congregational Church's garden in Fair Haven, Vermont, invite the children to help, and use the seeding and tending of the plants as an informal opportunity to teach Scripture. Some Bible gardeners insist that, at a minimum, the plants chosen should include the seven that are mentioned in Deuteronomy—wheat, barley, figs, pomegranates, dates, olives, and grapes—because these were so important in the Israel of the Old Testament. Many of these plants, however, are difficult to maintain in northern climates and are often omitted.

It is also common for biblical gardens to include a designated meditation area, where the visitor can reflect on the inspirational beauty of the display. A number of organizations have been established to help budding biblical gardeners learn about the varieties of plants they might include, along with sources where seeds may be obtained and instructions for design, seeding, and maintaining the display. A particularly useful online resource is www.biblicalgardens.org, which serves as a clearinghouse for all things related to Bible gardens.

The opportunities for creative expression are nearly endless, given the fact that there are more than 125 species of plants specifically mentioned in the Old and New Testaments, and the would-be gardener may choose any combination of them. Even those who live in climate zones that are less than hospitable to plants from the Mediterranean and Middle Eastern world can overcome the problem by creating a greenhouse garden.

The phenomenon of biblical gardens is growing rapidly, and churches of nearly every denomination have engaged in garden projects. The practice is gaining popularity throughout the world as well. A parallel trend in biblically inspired horticulture is also becoming increasingly common in Israel, although the tendency there is to focus specifically on Old Testament trees, herbs, flowers, and shrubs.

The Christian Cross

The symbol of the cross is an ancient one, far predating the rise of Christianity. It was employed by a variety of pagan religions and bore many different meanings. However, even though Christians throughout history have adopted folk traditions and symbols for their own use, the specific symbolism of the Christian cross was not derived in that way. It is a direct and explicit reference to the crucifixion of Jesus and the redemption of humankind.

Early depictions of the cross date as far back as the catacombs—the underground cemeteries used by Christians in the era of persecution. At that time, however, the use of the symbol was not generalized or particularly widespread. It was but one of many different symbols employed to denote the faith. It was only in the seventh century that the cross became the recognized symbol of Christianity. Over time, the form of the cross has been embellished in a number of different ways.

The Latin cross, a simple figure with a long vertical arm and a shorter crosspiece set above the midline, is also used by Protestant denominations. While the Catholic crucifix always includes a depiction of the Savior, specifically recalling the crucifixion, many Protestant groups keep it plain, preferring to emphasize the concept of resurrection. In medieval times, a cross with all arms of equal length was popularly employed on coats of arms. It denoted piety and faithfulness.

The Celtic cross, in which the cross figure is superimposed over a circle, dates back to the pre-Christian era and was once a pagan fertility figure. When used by Christians today, the original meanings have been obscured, and it is commonly used as a grave marker. Coptic Christians adorn the cross figure with stylized depictions of nails, to make the reference to the crucifixion even more direct. Perhaps the earliest cross symbol found in Christianity is the Greek cross, which was the one most often used until the seventh century. A plain figure, with all arms of the cross of equal length, it is found in many Christian places in the Mediterranean world. Regardless of the form used, however, the Christian cross bears the same meaning the world around: Christ has died for us, and He is risen!

Color Symbolism in Christianity

In all cultures, color is used to convey symbolic meaning, and each tradition assigns different values to different colors. For instance, in traditional China, red conveys purity, whereas white is the color of death—quite different from the values that we of the Western tradition would assign. In the Christian tradition, colors are often employed for symbolic purposes, even though they are almost never used this way in the Bible itself. In churches that celebrate more elaborate services, the colors are displayed in the vestments worn by the celebrant of the Mass, but they also appear in church decorations, banners, and Christian art.

The principle symbolic colors in the Christian tradition are black, blue, and brown; gray, green, and purple; and red and white. Yellow is also used, but more rarely than the others on the list. When they are used in the context of religious celebration, colors should be chosen with care. The most ominous color is, as one might expect, black. It signifies death, as well as sin and evil, both of which are associated with the death of the spirit. Brown is also generally assigned a negative meaning.

Like black, it can symbolize death, but it is also associated with degeneration and, by extension, with spiritual loss. Gray, on the other hand, is more hopeful. It is often used to symbolize repentance and therefore the hope of salvation.

Purple has many symbolic uses. Like gray, it can be used to express the concept of penitence, but it has also long been associated with the idea of royalty, and thus can signify power or strength. White represents purity, which is why it is the traditional color of the bridal gown. It is also associated with innocence, with the joys of childhood, and with grace. Silver is sometimes used to convey the same symbolic message as white.

Red, the color of blood, is associated with sacrifice. It is worn on the feast days of saints and martyrs in the Catholic and Anglican traditions to symbolize their suffering and sacrifice in service to the Lord. The symbolic meaning of yellow is more ambiguous than all these others. Associated with the rays of the sun, it can be interpreted as a positive symbol, and is sometimes used to connote divinity or holiness. Thus, in Christian art, depictions of Jesus, Mary, and the apostles often have a yellow or golden halo around their heads.

Blue and green are, symbolically speaking, the most positive of colors. Blue is associated with the sky and, by extension, with Heaven. It signifies spirit, truth, and hope. Paintings and images of Jesus's mother, Mary, often show her clothed in robes of blue and white. Green, the color of new growth in springtime, symbolizes growth and renewal, as well as spiritual rebirth and salvation of the soul. They invoke the idea of triumph over death, just as the new green shoots of plants represent the annual rebirth of the earth's bounty after its long winter sleep. Green has not always enjoyed acceptance as a symbolic color, particularly during its early years. It was rejected as being the color of paganism, and its use was banned.

Communion

During Jesus's last days on earth, He sat together with His disciples to take a final meal in fellowship. At one point in the meal, He took up a piece of the bread, showed it to His companions, and said, "This is my body." At the end of the meal, He raised his cup of wine and said, "This is the cup of the new covenant in my blood." He admonished His companions to eat and drink, "in remembrance of me." With these acts, Jesus established the commemorative rite of communion. In all Christian churches, all around the world, this ritual is reenacted every service.

When Jesus spoke these words, He was making a promise to His disciples and, by extension, to the Christian world to come. In the bread was symbolized the physical sacrifice He would face in a few short hours, but it also symbolized the resurrection to follow. In the wine was symbolized the promise He gave to His faithful, that their salvation was achieved through Him.

In the earliest days of the Church, the commemoration of Christ's life, death, and resurrection was accomplished through a full meal, shared in fellowship with one's small community of fellow believers. The celebration was conducted privately, because open displays of faith were punishable by death in those times. As the Church grew in size, however, the celebration of communion could no longer be done on such a small scale. By the third century, it had been made part of a larger commemorative service, and the elements of the meal were stripped down to just the most symbolically powerful: the sharing of the bread and wine.

Whenever the communion is offered, the story of Jesus's Last Supper is reenacted. But the symbolic meaning of the rite goes much further. At its heart is the fundamental concept of Christ's abiding love for humankind, so great that He was willing to lay down His life to secure our salvation. It is also symbolic of Spirit, which the communicant receives into his or her very body, a gift from God. It symbolizes the perfection of Christ's sacrifice on the cross, the redemption He achieved for us through that sacrifice, and it allows us to express our eternal gratitude and remembrance of these things. Along with baptism, it is one of the two central symbolic rites that are essential to the very existence of the Christian Church.

The Peacock, Praying Hands, and Good Shepherd

During the early church, when any public expression of Christian faith was likely to earn a swift arrest and execution, believers were forced to practice their religion in secret. Still, fellowship was an important element of Christianity, right from the beginning. In life, they gathered together in each other's homes to share the gift of faith. Even in death, the idea of Christian community was strong. They created the catacombs, where the dead could lie together, in silent fellowship.

To communicate to one another, for instance, to call fellow believers together for a shared communion meal, the early Christians had to find a means of covert communication—a code, so to speak, that identified them to one another. Similarly, in the cemeteries, there was a strong need to leave behind markings that identified the dead as believers in

Christ. For safety's sake, however, the meaning of the symbols used could not be obvious to outsiders.

Three early symbols of Christianity were chosen because they spoke clearly to fellow believers, but were likely to be misunderstood or overlooked by nonbelievers. These were the peacock, the image of the praying hands, and the sign of the good shepherd.

The image of the praying hands is the most straightforward of the three. The hands, clasped together with fingers extended or intertwined (the image appeared in both forms) signified piety and devotion. Members of the church would recognize the distinctive pose of the hands as customary in Christian worship, whereas outsiders would see nothing of obvious religious import.

The image of the good shepherd, often carrying a lamb, appears frequently in areas of early Christian influence. The image refers to one of Jesus's favorite motifs during his ministry. He spoke frequently of His role as a shepherd caring for His flock and bringing them to the light of truth. To Christians, the symbolism was unmistakable. Still, it was also subtle enough to escape detection by Roman soldiers. After all, outside of Rome and a few other important cities, this was a largely agricultural world. Images drawn from that world were unlikely to be thought of as particularly religious in content, except among those who were in the know.

The most obscure symbol was the peacock, usually depicted with his tail fully fanned out behind him. This was a common, and powerful, symbol of Christ's resurrection. The symbolic meaning was derived from an unusual fact about this gaily feathered bird: when he sheds his feathers, new ones grow in that are even more bright and vivid than the ones that were lost. To Christians, this was a perfect metaphor for Jesus's life, death, and resurrection.

The Sign of the Fish and the Christogram

In addition to pictorial symbols, early Christians often employed code-like devices to represent their faith. Believers easily recognized the message hidden within anagrams or acronymic constructions, whereas outsiders would merely be mystified.

The Sign of the Fish was one such coded message. Sometimes, it took the straightforward form of a stylized drawing of a fish and was marked on a house lintel to declare "A Christian dwells here." Often, however, they would use the actual word for *fish*, taken from the Greek, because it formed a perfect acronym for *Christ*.

The Greek word for *fish* is *ichthus*. To a Christian, this forms the following acronym:

I = the first initial of Jesus's name, Iesus
CH = the first letter of Jesus's title, Christos
TH = the first letters of the Greek word theus (of God)
U = the first letter of the Greek word *uiou* (son)
S = the first letter of the Greek word *soter* (Savior)

By treating the word *ichthus* as an acronym, a Christian could express the phrase "Jesus Christ, Son of God, Our Savior."

The Christogram worked in a similar way. It used the first two letters of Christ's name (in Greek, the letters *chi* and *rho*), with one superimposed on the other. During the era of persecution in the first three centuries after the crucifixion, it was a common secret symbol of the church. It was openly displayed on the war banners of the emperor Constantine when, on the night before a major battle, he received the vision from Jesus that led to his conversion to the Christian church.

About the Author

ALLAN A. SWENSON is the author of more than fifty books published by Doubleday, Random House, Fawcett, Ballantine, Grosset & Dunlap, Citadel, Birch Lane, Lyons & Burford, Lyons Press, Adams Media, Alpha Books, Penguin, Kensington, and other national book publishers, and children's books for David McKay, Rodale, and Gannett Books, and speaks widely on all book topics. He has been a nationally syndicated newspaper columnist for twenty-five years for NEA/United Media, writing about gardening, nature, and the outdoors, and appearing in more than two hundred newspapers nationwide, and the author of hundreds magazine feature articles for *GRIT*, *Modern Maturity*, *Moneysworth*, *Boardroom*, *The Farmer's Almanac*, *Scandinavia USA*, *Den Danske Pioneer* and various other national, regional, and specialty magazines. He is a veteran member of the Overseas Press Club in New York City, and is affiliated with the National Press Club in Washington, D.C, and other press organizations in the United States and abroad, as well as being a member of the Garden Writers of America, among other professional organizations, and a life member of the Association of Former Intelligence Officers.